CLEAN AIR – CLEAN WATER FOR TOMORROW'S WORLD

Today man stands on the brink of self-destruction. Smog fills the air, choking our lungs and dimming the sun. Our rivers, our lakes, even our oceans, are fast being transformed into giant cesspools. What are the causes of this increasingly perilous situation? How can we reverse the tide of pollution and find new sources of pure water to supplement our dwindling supply before there is total ecological disaster? This book, essential reading for all those concerned that there be a tomorrow for the world, describes the enormous task before us and the many unusual and creative ways scientists are attempting to solve the pollution problem.

TOMORROW'S WORLD SERIES

Clean Air–Clean Water
for
Tomorrow's World

by Reed Millard
and the editors of
Science Book Associates

photographs

JULIAN
MESSNER NEW YORK

Published by Julian Messner, a Division of Simon
& Schuster, Inc.
1 West 39 Street, New York, N.Y. 10018. All rights
reserved.

Third Printing, 1972

Printed in the United States of America

ISBN 0-671-32377-6   Cloth Trade
ISBN 0-671-32378-4   MCE

Library of Congress Catalog Card No. 70-139087

ACKNOWLEDGMENTS

We wish to thank the many associations and organizations in government, education and private industry whose assistance has made this book possible. For their help in giving us access to files and reports, and for time generously spent in consultation, we are particularly grateful to many individuals associated with the following United States Government agencies:

Atomic Energy Commission, Bureau of Reclamation, Department of Agriculture, Department of Transportation, Environmental Science Services Administration, Federal Water Quality Administration, Fish and Wildlife Service, Forest Service, Geological Survey, National Air Pollution Control Administration, Office of Saline Water, Public Health Service and Soil Conservation Service.

CONTENTS

Clean Air for
Tomorrow's World

1

THE PRICE
of AIR POLLUTION

"The world will end with a cough, a wheeze, a mass gasp of emphysema. Or so it seemed last week."

Thus began a news-magazine account of the events of early August, 1970. If anybody had previously questioned that air pollution is a menace that threatens the comfort, health and very lives of millions of people on this planet, there was not much room for doubt after what happened during those frightening days.

In the United States, along the Atlantic coast from Boston to Atlanta, a gray haze hung over the land. In dozens of cities, choking fumes reddened eyes, irritated throats and made breathing a struggle. Emergency wards of hospitals were crowded. In New York, a first-stage pollution alert was declared, and in other East

The smog that hangs over these American cities—St. Louis, Denver, Chicago—is typical of the air pollution problem that confronts cities all over the world.

Coast cities worried officials prepared to issue orders that would stop traffic and keep people off the streets.

Across the globe, a "white smog" blanketed Tokyo. Children playing in a schoolyard began collapsing. Other citizens—some 8,000 of them—were treated in hospitals for "smog symptoms." Many people wore gauze masks, and hundreds of thousands patronized coin-operated oxygen machines.

Although the eastern United States and Japan suffered the most acute attacks, owing to unusual weather conditions that kept polluted air clamped over them, cities all over the world were experiencing the effects of chronic air pollution. In Sydney, sulfurous, foul-smelling fumes were nauseating the Australians. In Santiago, the Chileans could not see the towering, snow-covered Andes because of the pall of smoke that obscured the majestic peaks. In Saigon, the trees along the boulevards were withered and dying. And a bluish haze lay over Athens, where investigators reported that corrosive pollutants in the air were eating away the stones of the Acropolis. This ancient building, they found, has suffered more damage in the past 25 years than it did in the previous 2,500 years of its existence.

With the high price of air pollution apparent everywhere, it was clear that the 143,000,000 tons of pollutants annually poured into the air in the United States alone was taking an appalling toll. Even measured in terms of money, the bill is staggering; estimates run as high as $13 billion a year. And, of course, money is not a very good measure of the deteriorating quality of life in a world where the air becomes less breathable year by year.

The Atmospheric Enemy

Man cannot blame air pollution on nature, but weather conditions can certainly make it much worse. They can also help reduce the penalty for man's folly in releasing tons of harmful substances into the air he breathes. Whether it acts as friend or foe, there is nothing anyone can do to change the weather factors that affect air pollution. All the pollution fighters can do is learn to understand these factors and try, as speedily as possible, to stop air pollution at its sources—the smokestacks of industry and the exhaust pipes of automobiles.

Man's friend in the atmosphere is the movement of air—the horizontal motion of the winds, the vertical motion of rising warm air. Ordinarily both these kinds of air currents are at work, helping to make moderate air pollution bearable. However, when atmospheric conditions are such that air movement is slowed or stopped, disaster looms.

The air above any given region or city may be looked on as a giant mixing area in which pollutants are stirred up and diluted. Within this expanse of air, warm air rises, cooling as it climbs. The point at which cooling air meets with air of the same temperature determines what scientists call the "mixing depth," and at this point air stops rising, just as if it had hit against a solid ceiling.

In most places, under normal circumstances, this ceiling is quite high. Above New York and Chicago, for instance, it usually hovers at about 3,000 feet. Some areas have a much lower ceiling. In Los Angeles the mixing depth is often as little as 300 feet. The low ceiling of this unfortunate city was observed as long ago as 1542, when the Spanish explorer Juan Cabrillo dropped anchor in what is now the harbor for Los Angeles. He was astonished to see the strange behavior of the smoke of the many Indian campfires. Rising straight up for a few hundred feet, it stopped suddenly and spread out horizontally over the valley. Cabrillo promptly named the harbor "the Bay of Smoke."

Obviously, when the mixing depth is shallow, there is less air in which pollutants can be diluted. When they are confined in the smaller space, the result is smog—sometimes deadly smog. This lowering of the ceiling—or reduction of the mixing depth, whichever you want to call it—is brought about by the existence of what is called an *inversion layer,* a layer of warm air that puts a "lid" on the air under it.

When an inversion layer situation is brought into being by certain meteorologic or topographic conditions, the air near the ground is kept from rising, blocked by this lid. The pollutants are confined in a smaller space, increasing their concentration in the air that people must breathe. Inversions are a menace that can strike at an entire region, as did the one that created the East Coast smog of August, 1970.

The "black fog" that struck London in 1952 is, so far, the greatest air pollution disaster in history. For five dreadful days an inversion layer shrouded the city with

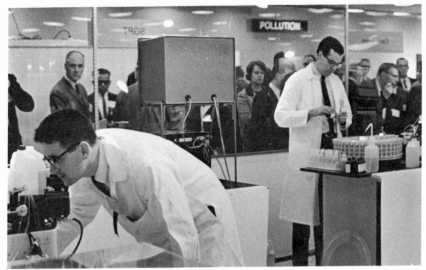

What does breathing pollutants do to people? Medical researchers are making blood tests to find out.

smog so thick that people literally could not see their extended hands. Traffic crawled, as policemen walked ahead of buses. Hospitals filled up. When the inversion finally lifted, 4,000 people had died from the effects of breathing the polluted air. Thousands more met premature deaths from the ordeal.

A similar inversion ten years later caused 750 deaths, a casualty list much smaller than that of the '52 crisis because of London's great strides in reducing pollution in the intervening decade.

New York City has had a series of inversions. Although they have not produced such high death tolls as the London smogs, they serve as grim warnings that modern cities can, at any time, become victims of a whim of the weather. In 1963 more than 400 deaths were caused directly by an inversion-created pollution crisis in New York. One in 1966 took 168 lives. Medical authorities are sure that casualties would have been much higher had the inversion not taken place on Thanksgiving weekend, when traffic was light and many factories were closed down.

What Air Pollutants Do to People

To stay alive, you need about 2.8 pounds of food and 4.5 pounds of water a day, but you must take in *30 pounds* of the substance you need more of than anything else— air. Breathing polluted air alters the body's responses to, and weakens its defenses against, infectious disease.

The respiratory tract is supplied with a marvelous disease defense mechanism. Cilia, tiny hairlike cells, line the respiratory passages. By their sweeping movement, they propel mucus, and the germs and dirt caught in it, out of the respiratory tract. Certain irritants, however, can slow down, or even stop, the action of the cilia. Pollutants can also constrict air passages and cause them to become clogged with mucus. They can make the cells that form the lining of the airways swell. They can even destroy cilia and other cells.

When this happens, breathing can become difficult, bacteria and other microorganisms are not removed as they should be and respiratory infection can result. Look at the findings of some typical medical investigations:

British doctors studied the health records of mailmen and found that absences for chronic bronchitis were three times greater when the men worked in heavily polluted areas.

In Los Angeles, when hospital records were checked, they showed that admissions for chronic and acute respiratory diseases went up in exact relationship to the degree of air pollution.

In Erie County, Pennsylvania, it was revealed that areas with the lowest amount of air pollution had the lowest hospital admissions for childhood asthma.

Other studies indicate that emphysema rates are *twice* as high in cities as they are in less polluted rural areas.

The pollutants that choke our atmosphere take two basic forms. They exist as gases, like the air with which they mingle, or as particulate matter, which is the name environmental scientists give to particles of liquids or solids.

Medical investigators have discovered that the particulates, which make up a large part of the pollutants in urban atmospheres (335 *tons* of them are produced on a winter day in New York City), play a sinister role in the bodily effects of breathing contaminated air. Particles of less than 2 or 3 microns (a micron is 1/25,000 of an inch) can reach deep into the lungs, getting past areas covered by mucus, which absorbs many gaseous chemicals. Thus, they act as carriers for dangerous chemicals which otherwise would not be lodged in the lungs.

The compounds in the witch's brew of pollutants in our air number in the thousands. However, to make things simpler, they are classified in broad groups as carbon and carbon oxides, hydrocarbons, sulfur dioxide and nitrogen oxides.

In the carbon group is plain ordinary *soot,* made up of carbon particles strung together in long chains. This

Particulate matter like this can be taken into human lungs, with disastrous results.

form of carbon attracts other chemicals, which cluster around it, creating a dangerous substance to breathe.

Another form of carbon is *carbon dioxide,* which is formed by combustion. Although it damages metal and stone, and may be playing a role in changing our climate, it is not considered a pollutant dangerous to human beings.

Carbon monoxide is a quite different matter. Odorless, colorless and tasteless, it does not contribute to the smog you can see, but it adds more than its share of menace. Higher concentrations of it than of any other gaseous pollutant are found in urban atmospheres. Laboratory experiments have shown that 100 parts per million—a concentration common in heavy traffic—can cause headaches and dizziness. Checks made inside automobiles on clogged freeways have produced counts as high as 237 parts per million.

A 1970 report of the National Air Pollution Control Administration revealed the dangers of carbon monoxide. Persons exposed to concentrations equal to those found in big cities during rush hours experience "an impairment of visual acuity and of perception of the passage of time." In a test sample of drivers who were "thought responsible" for accidents it was found that they had unusually large concentrations of CO in their blood.

"We don't know just what happens to a person who has continuous contact with high levels of carbon monoxide," a U.S. Public Health Service spokesman said. "The effects we found were due to reduced oxygen intake and were temporary, but that doesn't mean that

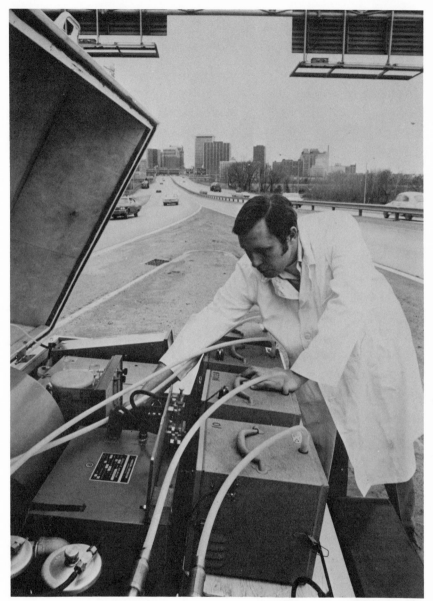

What kind of air do motorists breathe? Samples collected along an expressway reveal dangerous amounts of carbon monoxide and hydrocarbons.

there are no long-range effects. There is, for example, some evidence that an individual with a bad heart will be less likely to survive a heart attack if he has been exposed to consistently high CO levels."

Hyrdocarbons make up a huge family of chemicals—more than 1,000 different kinds. These substances are not harmful when they emerge from internal combustion engines and smokestacks. However, when they get into the air, sunlight reacts on them, turning them into other chemicals which are very dangerous. They include some that have shown alarming capability of producing cancer in laboratory experiments.

Sulfur dioxide is one of the most destructive pollutants in the chemical soup we breathe. A heavy, pungent, colorless gas when released into the atmosphere—mostly from industrial and home furnace sources—it goes to work to create a variety of other sulfur-based compounds that interfere with breathing.

Nitrogen oxides were long thought to be harmless. After all, you constantly take great quantities of nitrogen into your lungs, since it makes up some 78 per cent of air. However, when nitrogen combines with oxygen, it forms other chemicals. One troublemaker is *nitric oxide,* which comes into being when combustion takes place at high enough temperatures to cause a reaction between the nitrogen and oxygen in the air.

Automobiles and power plants operate at these temperatures, and hence spew great quantities of this chemical into the atmosphere, where it helps create still another chemical, *nitrogen dioxide.* It is one pollutant you can see. Its yellow-brown color cuts visibility and, when it reaches a concentration of 1 to 3 parts per million, your nose can detect its unpleasantly sweetish odor. Its dangers to the body are just beginning to be explored.

A particularly worrisome pollutant formed by reaction with other chemicals in *ozone,* a form of oxygen having three atoms of oxygen in a molecule rather than the two in ordinary oxygen. That extra atom gives ozone some properties that make it possibly the most dangerous to human beings of all air contaminants. Breathing as little of it as 1 part per million can cause a variety of reactions, including severe headaches, coughing, fatigue and choking. So dangerous is it considered to be that in many cities the presence of .5 part per million calls for sounding a first pollution alert; 1 part per million calls for a second-stage alert; and 1.5 parts per million is the signal for a disaster alert, during which factories are closed down and all traffic is stopped.

Many other chemicals—hundreds of them, say the dismayed researchers—are contributing to the impact of polluted air on human physiology. Among them are a lot of substances you never thought you'd be drawing into your lungs.

Look at lead, for instance. Particles of lead, long identified as a poison destructive to human beings, are coming from the lead additives that give gasoline more energy. To be sure, you get a certain amount of lead in the food you eat, but your body retains, at the most, 10 per cent of it. Up to 50 per cent of the lead you get through your lungs is retained.

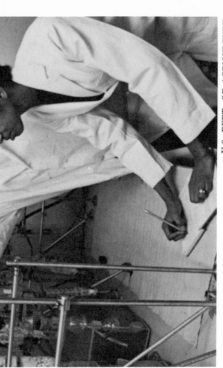

Food scientists in many laboratories are studying the effects of air pollutants on the nutritional value of foods.

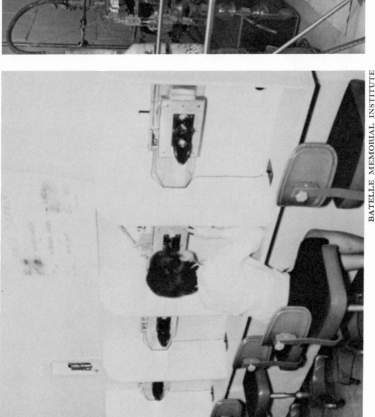

In this smog chamber the eyes of researchers are exposed to different smog mixtures.

And then there's arsenic, the well-known poison favored by writers of whodunits. A variety of agricultural sprays and industrial processes are adding arsenic to the air we breathe.

Another is asbestos. Now who would think that the average person would actually be inhaling asbestos? Yet studies show that quantities of asbestos dust are getting into urban air—some from construction projects, but most from the brake linings of automobiles. Long classed as an industrial poison, leading to lung cancer in workers in asbestos factories, the asbestos dust is now attacking city dwellers.

These are just some of the poisons that are being inhaled by people living in today's urbanized world.

What Air Pollution Does to Plants

One day, in the spring of 1970, lumberjacks moved into a stand of Ponderosa pines in the San Bernardino Mountains near Los Angeles. These towering rough-barked trees were under the protection of the U.S. Forest Service, but the snarl of power saws was soon followed by the crashing of forest giants that had taken over one hundred years to grow there. Forest rangers stood by, watching the process of denuding the forest they had so long guarded.

The lumbermen were there by invitation, for the trees were doomed long before the chain saws bit into them. They had been attacked by the deadly fumes of smog from the exhausts of automobiles in the urban sprawl of southern California. The needles on the pines had turned brown and fallen off, leaving bare branches as the trees died.

The majestic trees of San Bernardino National Forest are only some of the botanical casualties of the polluted air that ravages plants, just as it does other living creatures. Near every big city in the United States, and in many parts of the country distant from cities, plant life is suffering. In New Jersey, scientists have found that smog has injured at least 35 different kinds of plants. The U.S. Department of Agriculture reports that virtually every kind of agricultural crop has been hurt by pollutants in the air, and that crop losses run as high as $500,000,000 a year. Damage in California alone is put at $100,000,000 a year.

In the case of the Ponderosa pines of California, destruction came about indirectly. When ozone in the polluted air caused a breakdown in the normal process of photosynthesis, by which sunlight changes plant chemicals into nutrients, the trees were unable to produce the pitch which protects them from insects. They therefore fell easy prey to bark beetles and other pests.

To understand damage to other kinds of plants, you should remember that plants "breathe." Plant leaves are equipped with stomata, which, when you examine a leaf closely, appear to be tiny holes. Actually, the stomata are breathing tubes. When it is warm, stomata open and water vapor escapes from them into the air. (This process is called *transpiration*.) When the air temperature drops, the stomata in the plant close and the plant loses water vapor more slowly. Through these breathing tubes, the plant can take in poisons in the air, absorbing them into its system.

In this way plants are particularly subject to damage from sulfur dioxide. This has long been noted around copper smelters, where the smoke belching from stacks left a ghastly scarred desert of vegetation for miles downwind. Alfalfa, barley, cotton and grapes are some of the crops that have been severely damaged by sulfur dioxide.

Another chemical that enters the plant through the stomata is *fluoride*. Leaves subjected to this volatile substance turn brown around the edges. Apricot and peach trees are particularly injured by fluoride attacks, but all kinds of plants suffer when they receive large doses of fluorides from factories.

The choking smog that blankets cities, coming largely from automobile exhausts, affects plants by a somewhat different process. The stomata which provide the plant with its life-giving carbon dioxide close up. Growth of the plant is slowed, in some cases so much that it shrivels and dies.

Tiny amounts of some particularly virulent smog components are injurious to certain kinds of plants. For instance, *ethylene,* which is one of the substances emitted in automobile exhausts, has a startling effect on flowers. If present in quantities as small as 2 or 3 parts per billion, it can make certain flowers wither and drop off.

Researchers are constantly making disturbing new discoveries about the effects of air pollutants on plants. U.S. Department of Agriculture scientists, for instance, were puzzled by the fact that plants appeared to be suffering damage from ozone and sulfur dioxide at times when the concentrations of these substances were considered too low to be affecting the crops as much as they were. Tobacco, of all common plants the one most sensitive to ozone, became flecked with yellow when the amount of ozone present was only 2 parts per hundred million. (This ratio can be represented by one grain of salt in 1,600 gallons of water!) This was an astonishing discovery because, in the field, tobacco plants had never shown sensitivity to amounts smaller than 5 parts per hundred million. Other plants showed effects of sulfur dioxide when it was not present in amounts considered large enough to bother plants.

Laboratory experiments provided the answer. The two pollutants were teaming up to produce an effect that neither of them had alone in such small quantities. Thus, the researchers had discovered an even greater danger to plants than they had thought existed.

Air pollutants that damage plants have an effect on animals too, particularly on livestock eating vegetation which has absorbed dangerous chemicals. Cattle pastured near factories have sickened and died. Certain industrial processes emit fluoride, which some plants absorb, building up quantities of it in their leaves. While small amounts of fluoride are harmless to animals, they get a tremendous overdose when eating these plants. The result is abnormal, crippling bone growth. Scientists have observed many effects of pollution on animals, not only as a result of eating contaminated plants but also from breathing polluted air. Chickens have been shown

Air pollution can injure plants. Laboratory tests show what effects different chemicals have.

to lay fewer eggs, cows to produce less milk and sheep to grow thinner coats of wool.

Air Pollution Attacks Materials

Behind the Metropolitan Museum in New York stands a 69-foot-high pillar of stone, the obelisk called Cleopatra's Needle. It was fashioned by artisans over 3,000 years ago and brought to America a hundred years ago. In the single century during which it has been one of the sights of New York, the obelisk has suffered more damage than it did in the more than 30 centuries it existed in Egypt. What has attacked it is the corrosive air of Manhattan, which is eating away its stone and blurring the hieroglyphics with which it is adorned.

This is only one minor piece of evidence that air pollution strikes not only at people, animals and plants but at materials as well. The chemicals that contaminate the air make virulent attacks on cloth, paper, wood and metal. Few materials are safe from their ravages.

The Library of Congress says that, in spite of air conditioning, valuable books and manuscripts are disintegrating. The problem is that sulfur dioxide in the atmosphere is absorbed by the paper. Influenced by the presence of moisture, this compound turns to sulfuric acid, which injures the fibers in the paper and makes them brittle. Art galleries in all big cities are worried about the effect of polluted air on paintings. The Louvre, the Metropolitan Museum of Art in New York and the National Gallery of Art in Washington all report "irreparable damage" to valuable works of art.

Air pollution's assaults on stone are damaging not only such ancient buildings as the Acropolis in Athens and the Colosseum in Rome but much newer buildings as well. Cities are literally being eaten away by the various chemical processes arising from gases and particulates in the air. The effect of dirty, sooty air on buildings has long been noted, but only in recent years has the actual crumbling of stone occurred.

Many kinds of metals are the victims of poisoned air. Scientists have found that iron corrodes 5 times as fast in polluted atmospheres as it would in clean air; zinc 15 times as fast; nickel 25 times; and steel, most affected of all, 30 times as fast.

Few materials escape the acid touch of air pollutants. All kinds of natural fibers—cotton, wool, silk—are weakened by contact with chemical-laden air. Rubber is dried out and made brittle. Paint cracks and peels.

It is hard to measure the destruction of property resulting from polluted air's attacks on materials, but one study made in New Jersey gives some idea of its cost in dollars. It was calculated that, averaged out among the populace, the expense came to $200 a year for every person living in the area!

Does Air Pollution Affect the Weather?

Weather Bureau scientists were puzzled as they examined the reports that came in from La Porte, Indiana. There was something strange about the records sent in by a weather observer in this town, which is about 50 miles from Chicago. At times when nearby places had been experiencing clear weather, the La Porte readings repeatedly indicated heavy rainfall and thunderstorms.

An investigation provided a surprising explanation. This particular area had a special "climate" of its own. Air pollution was modifying the weather in La Porte. The meteorologists found the source in the smokestacks of Gary and Chicago. As towering plumes of smoke arose from them, raindrops formed around the billions of nuclei in the smoke. Wind patterns caused these rain clouds to move in the direction of La Porte, giving it, over a five-year period, 31 per cent more rainfall, 38 per cent more thunderstorms and 246 more days on which hail fell than places on either side of the polluted air stream.

Up to the time of these findings, in 1965, scientists had not been much concerned that air pollution might change the pattern of rainfall and increase the number of storms. But now, in many parts of the world, research programs are revealing the fact that the La Porte situation is not unique. Dr. Vincent Schaefer, the pioneering weather scientist who discovered that cloud seeding can create man-made rainfall, believes that many violent rainstorms have been produced by streams of pollutants.

The worst culprit in changing the weather is not the belching smokestack, the weather scientists assert, but high-flying jet aircraft. One study traces abnormally heavy, erratic rainfall to the concentration of tiny crystals in jet contrails. More commonly, the false cirrus clouds they form, high in the atmosphere, are creating gray, sunless days over many North American and European cities.

Can carbon dioxide produced by combustion products change the climate? Scientists aren't sure.

If commercial supersonic aircraft start flying, the clouds of crystals they would leave behind at very high altitudes might have an even greater effect on weather phenomena. A study by the Atmospheric Sciences Research Center in Albany, New York, makes the estimate that a fleet of 500 SSTs would dump 150,000 tons of water vapor into the atmosphere every day. Since this would hang suspended for years, it would cut off sunlight over large areas. Strangely enough, far from making the earth beneath it cooler, this might have the effect of making it warmer, for heat normally radiated back from the earth would be held in.

The climatic effect of pollutants that concerns scientists the most is such possible alterations in the heat balance of the earth. Our earth may be looked upon as

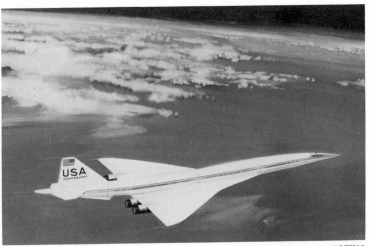

BOEING

Fleets of SSTs flying high in the stratosphere would produce quantities of water vapor. This is another form of air pollution which, say many scientists, could change the climate of the world.

a kind of heat machine, with the heat supplied, of course, by the sun. Every day the sun delivers to the earth an amount of energy equal to that which would be provided by burning 560 *billion* tons of coal. Some 30 per cent of this radiation that reaches the earth is reflected back into space. The total heat absorbed by the earth must balance the amount given off; otherwise, the earth would be getting steadily hotter or cooler. Actually, over a long period of time, it has remained at about the same temperature.

What will happen, scientists wonder, if pollutants released into the atmosphere should drastically upset this heat balance? If the pollutants kept the heat in, preventing it from being radiated back, the temperature of the earth would rise. If, on the other hand, the pollutants kept radiation from reaching the earth, the result could be a cooling of our planet.

Researchers have found that there is a strong possibility that *both* of these effects can be created by air pollutants. The chemical that would keep radiation in is carbon dioxide, which is given off by the combustion of fossil fuels. The amount of it in the atmosphere has been increasing steadily. Measurements show that in one four-year period the amount went up by 1.13 per cent, or 3.7 parts per million. Earlier studies reveal that the amount of CO_2 has been going up steadily since 1860, when the first efforts were made to measure it. Studies by Environmental Science Services Administration scientists show that worldwide mean temperatures are also rising. They found that the greatest rise is in the northern hemisphere, where the greatest amounts of combustion occur. Climatologists are cautious about blaming this temperature rise on CO_2, but many say there is a strong possibility that the blanket of this gas could eventually raise earth temperature enough to melt the polar ice caps and flood the seacoasts of the world.

The other pollutant that may have an effect on climate is also a product of combustion—particulate matter. Tiny particles, floating in space, have the opposite effect of CO_2. Sunlight striking them is reflected back into space, and therefore does not reach the earth. Large enough amounts of particulate matter circulated in the atmosphere could reduce earth temperature enough to produce gradual cooling. This in turn could result in an increase in the ice caps and could conceivably bring on another ice age.

"Perhaps we'll be lucky enough to have these two effects cancel each other out," suggests Dr. Schaefer, "but we shouldn't count on it. We'd better keep a careful watch on what might just be the highest price we'll pay for air pollution—flooded cities or an ice-covered land."

Scientists have another worry about what pollution may do to the weather. If we build and fly the controversial faster-than-sound aircraft, the SSTs, these planes will fly at high altitudes, around 70,000 feet, where water vapor from their engines will stay suspended. This could, some experts believe, create a "greenhouse" effect, with the blanket of vapor not letting heat escape from the earth. A few planes would not have too much effect, but if large numbers of them were flying regularly, the amount of vapor would be great. Dr. Vincent Schaefer, of the Atmospheric Sciences Research Center at Albany, New York, calculates that a fleet of 500 SSTs would produce 150,000 tons of vapor a day.

An even more worrisome possibility is that water vapor might interfere with a chemical process that takes place in the upper atmosphere. In this process ordinary oxygen is turned into ozone. This ozone in turn intercepts ultraviolet radiation which, if it reached the earth, would be damaging to life processes.

Whether the SSTs are actually such a menace is not certain. Much more research has to be done before scientists know for sure. However, we must pay attention to the possibility that this technological advance in transportation could add another costly item to the high price of air pollution.

2

CRACKDOWN on CARS
THAT POISON the AIR

When 39 unusual automobiles lined up on the campus of Massachusetts Institute of Technology one day in August, 1970, they dramatized the most pressing of all air pollution problems—what to do about the poisonous exhausts of the present-day automobile. Many of the vehicles entered in the Clean Air Car Race looked like ordinary 1970 models, but, in one way or another, all were different. Each of them was propelled by some form of power that engineers hoped would keep the car of tomorrow from punishing the atmosphere and the lungs of human beings.

In the race, which took the cars over a course running from MIT, in Cambridge, Massachusetts, to the campus of Cal Tech, in Pasadena, California, some 3,600 miles away on the course followed, there were cars that burned alcohol, natural gas and jet fuel. Some were powered by turbines, others by electric motors. (There was no steam car actually in the race because those entered failed to qualify under the rules, which called for the capability of traveling at a speed of at least 45 miles per hour.)

The agencies participating in the Clean Air Car Race represented the various elements of society which must cooperate if we are to defeat the air pollution problem the gasoline powered internal combustion engine presents: *government,* through a grant from the U.S. Public Health Service; *industry,* through test cars and research equipment in a number of the entries; *science,* represented by the research staffs of the many universities involved; *citizens,* represented by the students who did much of the work in engineering the cars and who drove them on their grueling cross-country test.

The internal combustion engine, the sturdy, dependable motive force that created the automobile age, has turned out to be the most menacing of air polluters. In a single year, 1970, automobiles poured over *ninety million tons* of pollutants into the atmosphere of the United States. Nationally, the automobile accounts for 60 per cent of all the contaminants that get into the air. Locally, in many urban situations, it makes up as much as 90 per cent. In New York City alone, automobiles spew out 4,000 tons of waste chemicals every day. In Los Angeles that figure is more than doubled, at 9,400 tons a day.

Engineers examine a thermal muffler, a device that burns exhaust pollutants of automobiles.

The pollutants in exhaust gases are analyzed by technicians seeking ways to reduce the dangerous emissions of the internal combustion engine.

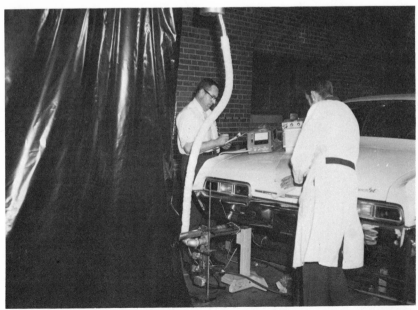

Cleaning Up Today's Cars

The trouble is that, without air pollution controls, the internal combustion engine operates in a way that is bound to pollute the atmosphere. The exhaust gases resulting from the explosion of the gasoline-air mixture in the cylinders contain carbon monoxide, hydrocarbons and nitrogen oxides. In addition, pollutants get into the air from the crankcase, from which evaporated lubricating oil and some exhaust escape. Unburned gasoline that evaporates from the carburetor after the engine is stopped also adds to air pollution.

Devices have been installed on 1970 cars that keep some of the pollutants from reaching the air. Unfortunately, they fall far short of bringing emissions to the standards set for 1975 by the Department of Health, Education and Welfare. With present devices, the carbon limit per mile is set at 2.2 grams; by 1975 that must be reduced to .05 grams. Carbon monoxide, which now can be emitted at 23 grams per mile, must be reduced to 11 grams by 1975. Nitrogen oxide, presently allowed at 3 grams, must be cut to .9 gram.

Obviously, the car makers have a long way to go, but some are optimistic about the progress they are making. They have come out with various "clean air packages" which they hope will make internal combustion engines acceptable. A modified Ford-made Capri, which was the over-all winner in the Clean Air Car Race, managed to cross the country and stay within the 1975 standards. In fact, it did even better, meeting some tougher rules projected for 1980.

The auto companies pin their hopes on two promising pieces of equipment—the catalytic muffler and the thermal reactor. The catalytic muffler is really a small chemical factory in which a catalyst reacts with the exhaust gases, changing them to harmless carbon dioxide and water. Researchers have been working on such a muffler for more than 20 years, and have found that it presents many problems. The mufflers themselves are expensive—they would cost at least $100—and the catalysts, which would "wear out" and have to be replaced at frequent intervals, are also costly. However, greatly speeded up research has helped engineers hurdle some of the obstacles. Lowers costs for mufflers and longer life for catalysts may at last be possible.

The thermal reactor is actually a furnace. The exhaust gases, hot from the engine, are fed into it. Oxygen is added to the hot gases, causing them to oxidize—that is, to burn. The gas emerging is mostly harmless. The trouble with the thermal reactor is that the furious heat required calls for the use of special metals, which would be very expensive.

A big step toward use of the catalytic muffler is taking the lead out of gasoline. The lead additives in gasoline, which improve the performance of cars, were disastrous in experimental mufflers. The lead affected the catalyst and soon made it stop working. Without the lead in gasoline, it will function much better. The 1971-model cars are made to operate on unleaded gas, which is being offered by all major oil companies.

Many scientists are sure it's going to take a lot more than just removing the lead from gasoline to solve the automobile pollution problem. The emissions from un-leaded gasoline will be different, all right, but there is a possibility that the chemicals they pour into the atmos-phere will prove dangerous.

As an American Petroleum Institute engineer says, "It's a whole new show—and we may find ourselves deal-ing with a lot of unknowns."

With all the problems connected with burning gaso-line, why not cut right around it and find some other fuel?

That's what many researchers are trying to do. The most likely one they've found is natural gas. Internal combustion engines adapted to use it have been found to emit only a fraction of the pollutants that come from gasoline. A gas company in southern California which operates a fleet of cars with natural gas found that car-bon monoxide was reduced by 90 per cent, hydrocarbons by 65 per cent and oxides of nitrogen by 50 per cent. With special engines and better mufflers, natural gas might become almost pollution-free.

Before it could be widely used, however, researchers will have to lick a tough problem: how do you carry the stuff? To provide enough natural gas to deliver the energy equivalent to that in a tank of gasoline, a tank at least twice as large as today's tanks must be provided. Students who designed one of the cars entered in the Clean Air Car Race of 1970 ingeniously used scuba divers' air tanks, but the number of them required filled the entire trunk.

Whatever devices or fuels are adopted in efforts to clean up the internal combustion engine, the dollars-and-cents costs of modification will be high. Some estimates run as high as $350 per car for special mufflers and as high as $400 for special tanks and adaption that will permit burning natural gas.

Motorists who pay this high first cost, which will, of course, be added to the price tags of cars, may be reluctant to pay the additional costs of servicing the new devices. Frequent checkups may be required to keep them in proper working order. A study of recent model cars in Arizona showed that within one year after the cars came off the assembly line 50 per cent of the emission control devices were not working properly. A test made with 333 rental cars, which were routinely given proper servicing, revealed that 53 per cent failed to meet hydrocarbon and carbon monoxide control standards after only 11,000 miles of driving.

Fume-Free Cars for Tomorrow

No one can safely predict that the many approaches to cleaning up the internal combustion engine will save it. Many researchers are convinced that, no matter what is done to it, it will still be a fume maker that will have to be replaced by some other type of engine.

All major auto makers, and a number of independent companies, are working on alternatives. Besides these commercial efforts, a Government program is being carried out by the Division of Motor Vehicle Research of the U.S. Department of Health, Education and Welfare. This agency expects to spend $50,000,000 to develop a new low-pollution power plant for automobiles.

"If the auto industry fails to meet the standards by

An engine like this one being tested is designed to recharge batteries in a hybrid electric car.

1975," says John Brogan, the engineer in charge of the project, "we will have an engine ready and the industry will have little choice but to switch."

The engineering problems that stand in the way of perfecting a power plant to compete with the internal combustion engine are formidable. Each type of engine, it seems, has its own set of difficulties.

Turbine. Automobile makers have been at work for many years on this type of engine, which is so simple in principle but has turned out to present many developmental difficulties. In a turbine engine, a compressor feeds compressed air into a chamber; fuel is added and ignited by an electric spark. The hot burning gases strike the blades of the turbine, which is geared to the driving wheels of the vehicle. In the process, most of the pollutants are burned up in the combustion chamber and never reach the air.

As far back as 1954, Chrysler Motors had produced a workable turbine and, in the early '60s, actually installed turbines in 200 cars which were test driven by ordinary drivers under day-to-day conditions. The difficulties that showed up were poor acceleration and low mileage. From the standpoint of engineers looking at its antipollution qualities, it also falls short of perfection. The turbine auto engine is a metallurgist's nightmare because it has to operate at extremely high temperatures. At anything short of 3,000° F., close to the melting point of steel, it does not operate very efficiently and will emit large amounts of nitrogen oxide, although its emission of carbon monoxide and hydrocarbons is low.

The motor makers have not given up on turbines, however. General Motors and Ford are both making them for trucks and buses. A technologic breakthrough that licks the nitrogen oxide problem could put the turbine into tomorrow's automobile.

Steam. The obstacles in the way of turning to steam seem even greater than those that have stalled the turbine. Offhand, steam propulsion has many advantages. Since it is an external combustion engine, burning its fuel outside the power-producing part of the engine, a steam engine burns much more completely than does an internal combustion engine. The combustion in the miniature furnace which heats the water or other liquid which drives the pistons of a steam engine does not leave unburned portions of the fuel to be sprayed into the

Students at the University of California at San Diego built the box-like steam engine that powers this car, which was designed as an entry in the Clean Air Car Race of 1970.

atmosphere, nor does it create new chemicals which can react with the air. In one extensive test, a steam engine was shown to have released less than 1 per cent of the pollutants emitted by a standard automobile engine.

With obvious advantages luring them on, researchers for the major auto makers, as well as for scores of smaller concerns, are trying to beat the problems of steam cars. These problems center on efficiency and performance equal to that of the established internal combustion engine. Steam cars so far developed fall far short of being production models that would satisfy the American motorist.

Electric. The electric car has a long history. Production models were made right up to 1929. Many experts are predicting that they will make a comeback and prove to be the ultimate answer to the pollution-free car.

The simplest form of electric car uses batteries, which power an electric motor, which turns a driveshaft. Another way to use the electricity is to have smaller electric motors, one to power each wheel. The catch is that up to 1970, nobody had found a battery that could meet all the specifications of weight, cost, dependability, power and length of life.

The struggles of battery-powered electric cars entered in cross-country "Clean Air" races illustrate some of the problems. In the 1968 race, troubles for these cars came in the form of burned-out motors, overloaded circuits, popping fuses and batteries so sizzling hot they had to be packed with chunks of ice. It takes from 10 to 50 batteries to power most electric cars of present design.

A small, pollution-free electric bus. The electric propulsion system that powers this 24-passenger vehicle could be used for large buses—or the family car.

In one model, these batteries weighed 2,000 pounds. Adding so much weight to a car sets up an unfortunate cycle. To get enough power to move the extra batteries, you have to add more batteries.

Many new types of batteries, which may solve this problem, are being developed. Instead of using the chemical reaction between lead plates (which are naturally heavy) and sulfuric acid, these new batteries substitute other metals for the plates and other chemicals to provide the reaction. One new battery, using aluminum and sulfur-sodium, has 15 times the power of an ordinary battery. A single such battery could carry a full-sized car 200 miles between charges.

Keeping even superbatteries of the future charged is a difficulty that challenges the engineers. To be acceptable, an electric car would have to hold a charge great enough to provide at least the number of miles a tankful of gasoline will drive an internal combustion car. This mileage has been achieved in some experimental batteries.

Even if batteries run a long time, there is still the problem of recharging them. Various schemes have been proposed. One of them is to provide electrical outlets in parking meters, garages and driveways, where the motorist can plug in a battery charger. Another calls for exchanging batteries at service stations. A lift would whisk the run-down batteries out of your car and replace them with fully charged ones. In any case, replacing gasoline-powered engines with batteries entails setting up a whole new servicing system, which in itself presents immense problems.

Hybrid Electric. To get around the problem of frequent battery recharges, engineers have come up with the hybrid electric car, which uses an engine of some kind to charge up the batteries. Various types of engines have been developed which, while they emit some pollutants, don't produce anything like the quantities emitted by an engine that provides the power to propel a car.

One successful experimental model employed a small, furnacelike external combustion engine to charge the 20 batteries that provided electric power for the car when it was driven in urban areas. An objection to the charge-as-you-go hybrid electric is the fact that it is bound to be heavy, with the combined weight of the

batteries and the engines. Also, it tends to be compli-
cated, since it has two power systems.

Fuel Cell Electric

"Fill her up with hydrogen." This may be the order
you'll be giving when you drive a kind of car that, many
authorities think, will be the eventual winner in the com-
petition to find the best way to use electricity. Hydrogen
might be one of the fuels used to power the fuel cells
of this car of the future.

Actually, the fuel cell is an old invention. Some 20
years before the present-day lead-acid battery was invented, Sir William Groves, an English scientist, discovered a new kind of self-renewing battery, one in which
a chemical reaction continued to produce electricity as
long as fuel and oxygen were provided. What takes place
inside a fuel cell is an electrolytic reaction that produces
a steady flow of current.

Modern descendants of Groves's pioneering fuel cell
use a variety of fuels, including hydrogen and oxygen,
and are powering such varied vehicles as golf carts,
research submarines, satellites and spacecraft.

Putting them into automobiles is a tempting goal for
the pollution fighters because the fuel cells emit no harmful fumes. A fuel cell is smaller than an ordinary battery,
and it can come in a variety of shapes, which means that
the 20 to 40 cells which might be required could be fitted
into odd places, such as body panels, roofs or under the
floor. Tanks for the fuel are another problem, however.
At present, ones large enough to hold hydrogen, which

seems like one of the more desirable fuels, are bulky and cancel out the value of the fuel cells' compactness.

There are many problems that block the various ways of using electricity to power automobiles. Some pessimists are afraid that it will take a long time to overcome them. They predict that it will be 25 years before any kind of electric car can offer the performance expected of a full-sized family car for highway driving. However, long before then, an electric car for more limited purposes can surely be built. It would serve for short hauls, close-to-home shopping trips and other in-town driving. And certainly the fight on urban pollution can be helped along by using electrically powered delivery vehicles in downtown districts.

Modified internal combustion engine, turbine, steam, electric—no one can predict which will win out as the automobile of the future. The only certainty is that the fume-belching car of today has to be ruled off the road.

A way of fighting automobile pollution that has aroused the hopes of many environmentalists is to decrease use of the automobile, substituting some form of mass transit. This scheme has some possibilities, but mass transportation systems have a long way to go before they can convince many motorists that the flexible, door-to-door personal transportation provided by the automobile should be given up. Many surveys indicate that a vast majority of today's motorists have a strong resistance to using any form of public transit.

Can this resistance be overcome? Many experts believe it can. They point to such advanced transportation

Air cushion vehicles that can travel hundreds of miles an hour on the surface, or . . .

. . . Gravity Vacuum trains travelling equally fast deep underground are advanced forms of pollution-free transportation that can lure passengers away from automobiles.

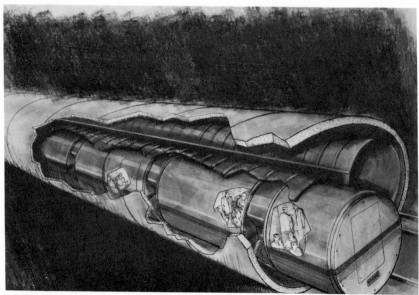

systems as BART (Bay Area Rapid Transit), serving the San Francisco-Oakland area. This 78-mile network of surface and sub-surface automated trains can carry 100,000 people an hour. Clean and silent, they move at speeds of 80 miles an hour. Passengers using BART can reach their destinations in a fraction of the time that it takes to go by automobile over congested freeways and bridges.

Many other cities around the world are constructing or planning such modern transportation systems. Since they all use electricity, in themselves they create no pollution. (The power plants that make the electricity are, as we shall see, a different matter.)

Improved high-speed transportation systems between cities also hold promise of getting some cars off the road. On Japan's Tokaido Line—"the fastest railroad in the world"—trains flash along the tracks at 130 miles an hour. In the United States, the Turbo Train, operating between New York and Boston, and the Metroliner, running between New York and Washington, demonstrated in the late 1960s that trains can be moved faster and that they can attract passengers.

Many much more advanced developments promise far greater use of mass transit. One of them is GVT—Gravity Vacuum Transit—a system that would send trains hurtling through deep tunnels at speeds as high as 400 miles an hour. The tunnels dip down, enabling the trains to be propelled partly by gravity.

Another high-speed system would operate on the surface. Air cushion vehicles which move, not on wheels, but on cushions of air that lift them above their tracks, can achieve speeds of hundreds of miles an hour. These machines, already in use in Europe and now being tested at the Department of Transportation's test center near Pueblo, Colorado, are being studied to see how this form of transport can be applied.

Whatever systems of mass transport are worked out, few believe that they can result in more than a small drop in use of the automobile. Such a drop could help, especially in the years before pollution-creating vehicles can be ruled off the road. However, the time required to develop advanced systems is so great that it seems likely that, before they can get into operation, automobiles will have been cleaned up.

Perhaps an even more effective pollution-reducer will be the "autoless core"—an area in the heart of a big city where automobiles will not be allowed. Buses operating from parking areas around the fringes of downtown areas would carry the motorists the few miles to the city center. Such a scheme could help reduce the quantity of pollutants suspended in the air of downtown areas by as much as 50 per cent.

When all the plans are weighed and measured, however, environmental experts always come up with the conclusion that there is only one really good way to clean up automobile exhaust pollution, and that is to create a pollution-free automobile. That is the bright hope for the future that must be the aim of all who want to make the air in tomorrow's world fit to breathe.

3

FIGHTING the FUMES of INDUSTRY

Farmers near a metal plant in Tennessee complained that their crops were being blighted and their cattle and other livestock sickened by the fumes that poured out of the factory smokestacks. The company agreed that the farmers had a just complaint. But, engineers assured them, it wouldn't be necessary to close down the plant, as some angry citizens were urging, nor would the agriculturalists have to give up their farms.

Within a few months, an astonishing change had come to the air that had been ruining crops and injuring animals. Though the factory was still operating full blast, the air near it was now country fresh—so fresh that the company decided on a startling demonstration. In the fields right next to the factory, they set up a company-owned farm. There they pastured a herd of prize cattle, which continued to stay as healthy as cattle remote from any industry.

What happened at the Tennessee industrial plant is going to happen in more and more places. Science, engineering and industrial management are waging a successful fight on the poisons that once poured from factory chimneys. The many industrial processes—grinding, polishing, sanding, spraying, cooking and smelting—which have so long given rise to the dust and fumes that have blighted industrial areas can be controlled by tools and techniques already available. The pollutants from combustion of oil and coal still present problems, but new advances in science promise to clean up this trouble spot.

ALCOA

These healthy cattle, pastured close to a factory, show what industry can do to clean up the air.

Putting the Lid on Factory Fumes

Not long ago the high chimney was about the only means of combating pollution from factory fumes. Hot waste gases were sent up tall stacks and then released into the air, with the hope that the winds would spread them out harmlessly. That was often a vain hope, as engineers are still learning. For example, some tall new industrial stacks were recently built in the Ruhr, in Germany. They took the fumes away from that part of Germany, all right, but people in Norway and Sweden soon began to notice something they had never seen before—snow blackened by soot and chemicals.

Tall chimneys still have their place as a means of carrying off harmless substances and warm air. However, engineers now have many tools which they can use to keep air pollutants from ever getting out of the stacks. One commonly used device sprays exhaust gases with water. The water droplets become collecting points for particles which are flushed out of the gas. Another method uses centrifugal force. Gases are sent into a revolving cyclinder which throws particles in them against the wall, where they slide down and out the bottom of the chamber. An updraft carries the cleaned-up gas out the top of the cylinder.

Other devices use filters made of metals, plastics, fabrics and other materials to capture a variety of solid and gaseous pollutants. Many of the plants that once produced the most fumes, such as chemical and cement plants, use filter systems called "baghouses," in some installations many stories high. The gas enters at the open end of each bag (really a porous tube) and then moves out through the pores, depositing its particles on the inner surface. The bags are automatically shaken from time to time to remove the material thus retained in them.

The most versatile fume-stopper is the electrostatic precipitator. Gases are passed over high-voltage electrodes in collector plates. The electrodes give a charge to the particles, causing them to stick to the plates. In many situations, precipitators can remove 98 per cent of the pollutants.

If these devices are so effective, why do we have any industrial pollution at all? There is only one basic reason —cost. The pollution-reducers are expensive. One large

A giant collector at a metal plant catches fumes which could blight the countryside.

The cutaway illustration shows the size of the huge collecting plates used in electrostatic precipitators, which collect particles and fumes that would otherwise get into the atmosphere.

steel plant had to spend over $22,000,000 to install apparatus that stopped the clouds of noxious fumes that blighted the area around it. A single large precipitator can cost $1,000,000. A chemical filtering system installed by a pharmaceutical plant called for a $10,000,000 expenditure.

Compared with the cost of the machines to which they are attached, the cost of these devices doesn't seem so high. It cost $100,000 to add a baghouse unit to a $1,500,000 machine. Adding the units necessary to clean up a refinery, in which the various refining equipment cost $18,000,000, required less than $500,000.

On the other hand, in some industries the cost of anti-pollution equipment can exceed the cost of the basic machinery. In the steel industry, $200,000 scrubbers have been added to open hearth furnaces worth only $250,000.

Many industries have made the surprising discovery that antipollution equipment can more than pay for itself by salvaging valuable materials that were literally going up in smoke. A chemical processor salvaged chlorine at a profit of $20 a ton.

The fight the Los Angeles County Air Pollution Control District has successfully waged on industrial air pollutants shows what can be done when industry really puts to work all the devices at its disposal. Of the 14,000 tons of pollutants that entered the air in this southern California county in a single year, only 1,330 tons came from industrial sources. While this was admittedly too much, it was nevertheless small compared with previous levels, and with the 12,465 tons of pollutants that came from automobiles.

Before and after photos show that smokestacks don't have to pour out air-polluting smoke.

NATIONAL AIR POLLUTION CONTROL ADMINISTRATION

Many experts believe that when 80 per cent efficiency is achieved in controlling industrial fumes, air pollution levels from this source will not be a great danger. Others believe that there is no need to settle for this percentage. They are sure that with good monitoring systems, strict regulations, proper enforcement and cooperation from industry, as well as a reasonable amount of technological progress, we should be able to cut air pollution created by manufacturing processes by at least 95 per cent in tomorrow's world.

Power Without Air Pollution

Already the United States produces more electricity than the next four nations combined—Russia, Japan, the United Kingdom and West Germany. Yet what we produce now is only a start on the vast quantities we will need. In the next decade alone we will have to provide electricity equal to the amount the United States has used in all the time since Edison invented the electric light almost 100 years ago. Our use of electricity has been doubling every 10 years, but it will go up even faster in the future. Forecasters predict a 600 per cent increase over present use by the year 2000.

What does this have to do with air pollution? Plenty. Although electric power production accounts for only 13 per cent of the tonnage of pollutants that reach the air in 1970, it accounts for more than half of the sulfur dioxide and 27 per cent of the oxides of nitrogen. This is because most power is produced by fossil fuels, which emit the most pollutants, particularly the one that is hardest to control—sulfur dioxide.

Most power plants today get their energy from coal, a fuel which has begun to seem old-fashioned, since it is no longer used to heat homes. However, it is still the most abundant fuel we have. Geologists estimate that nearly half the world reserve of five thousand billion tons of coal is located in the United States. No wonder, then, that power producers turn to this black stone that burns, in spite of the 16,000,000 tons of sulfur dioxide that present-day power production pours into the atmosphere.

Sulfur can be removed from coal, and various research programs are working toward the day when huge chemical extraction plants will be set up at coal mine sites. Another scheme that may work out in the future calls for gasifying the coal in the ground. By this method engineers would set fire to the coal while it was still deep underground. As it burned, high temperatures would turn the energy in it into gas, which could then be piped to power plants, either at the site or some distance away. U.S. Bureau of Mines experiments in Gorgas, Alabama, and at other places, have proved that the system is not far from becoming practical. It could solve the pollution problem, because the gas that emerges from the underground fires is free of the troublesome sulfur dioxide.

What about other fuels, such as oil? Unfortunately, most oil found in the United States is high in sulfur content. The limited amount of low-sulfur oil found in this country, and that imported from other parts of the world, is desperately needed to fuel the oil-burning heating plants of homes, factories and public buildings. Efforts to comply with antipollution regulations in many cities created a frightening shortage of sulfur-free heating oil during the winter of 1970-71.

Sulfur can be removed from oil by chemical processes, and many oil-processing plants are being set up to accomplish this. However, getting the sulfur out is expensive, and it will be a long time before there are enough plants to make low-sulfur oil plentiful.

Sulfur can also be removed from the smoke given off by burning oil and coal by some of the same means used to remove other chemicals from factory fumes. However, any methods devised are expensive and may not be workable on a wide scale.

In 1970, a panel of the Academy of Engineers of the National Research Council declared flatly that ". . . a commercially proven technology for the control of sulfur dioxides from combustion processes does not exist." The engineers who made this statement hope that an experimental power plant going into operation in 1971 will prove them wrong. A special "scrubber" will remove 50 tons a day of raw sulfur and sulfuric acid from the stacks of a power station in Everett, Massachusetts. It is hoped that the $5,000,000 device being sponsored jointly by a utility company and the National Air Pollution Control Administration will reduce the irritating pollutant far below even the toughest standards.

Isn't there any fuel that doesn't emit the noxious SO_2? Yes, there is—natural gas. In fact, it doesn't give off many pollutants of any kind. The trouble is, we're burning this versatile fuel at the ruinous rate of more than nine trillion cubic feet a year in the United States. To be sure, we have a proven reserve of 200 trillion cubic feet underground, but there is no certainty that it can all be extracted economically. Some experts warn that we may run out of natural gas in a few years. Nuclear energy, in the form of underground blasts to "loosen" natural gas in certain deposits, might greatly increase our supply, but this technique is still experimental.

Can we get more power from hydroelectric plants? After all, using running water to turn turbines does not require combustion and contributes no pollutants to the air. This clean source of power does offer possibilities. Only about 12 per cent of all electricity in the United States now comes from such plants, and this percentage may drop in the future.

However, that does not mean that we will not find ways to make greater use of the energy in moving water to provide power for tomorrow. Such projects as the North American Water and Power Alliance (NAWAPA), which you will read about in a later chapter, could be a factor. There are other ways to tap the mighty rivers in remote parts of the continent. One such river is the Churchill, in Labrador. It is being harnessed by a gigantic dam that will bring into being the largest hydroelectric power system in North America when it goes into operation in the mid '70s. The mighty turbines will be driven by water dropping more than 1,000 feet, and will feed over 5,000,000 kilowatts of electricity into the power grids serving Canada and the northeastern United States. Compare this with the 1,250,000 kilowatts turned out by the giant Hoover Dam in Arizona-Nevada.

A technological advance that could greatly increase the amount of power we get from distant sources is the development of new systems of transmission. At the present time much power is lost in transmission through overhead power lines. Scientists foresee using supercold to transmit power without loss over thousands of miles. They would use underground tubes cooled by liquid hydrogen, which would bring the temperature down to −438° F. This would employ the phenomenon of superconduction, which allows electric current to flow indefinitely without loss of power.

Using such cryogenic transmission lines would have the desirable incidental effect of eliminating the overhead transmission lines that scar the landscape. All of the power requirements of New York City, for example,

Nuclear power plants like this one in New England pour out no air pollutants.

U.S. ATOMIC ENERGY COMMISSION

could be supplied by three cryogenic cables inside 18-inch pipes.

Can't we simply turn to the atom for our power? Many environmental scientists say that is just what we must do as rapidly as possible. Atomic energy creates electricity in the same way fossil fuels do—by producing heat. However, no combustion is needed. The fissioning of atoms creates the heat which turns water into steam, which drives the generators. There are no fumes, and, as stated by the Atomic Energy Commission, "the extremely small amount of radioactivity produced can be held and released in such tiny amounts and under such favorable conditions that it poses no health hazard whatsoever." Some of the newer plants release no fumes at all and are built without any kind of smokestack.

While there is no sulfur dioxide air pollution in routine operation of a nuclear power plant, many people, both scientists and laymen, fear a far more deadly menace. They visualize the possibility of a nuclear reactor in a congested area meeting with some kind of an accident, such as disruption by an earthquake, and emitting clouds of deadly radiation. So far no such dread event has occurred, although there have been mishaps in atomic plants. Most authorities are sure that there could be no explosion of the fissionable material in the plant, but the worry is there.

It is one problem that suggests that atomic energy, as now derived from fissioning atoms, may not be the final answer to stopping air pollution by our electricity producers. Moreover, nuclear power plants, like the fossil-

An experimental solar power installation uses mirrors to con-
centrate solar energy. The sun may prove to be the ultimate
source of pollution-free power.

fuel burners, do add to our water pollution problems.

There is no question about what we will use to provide clean-air electric power of the future if a dreamed-of breakthrough is made by the nuclear scientists. They hope that someday they will harness fusion, rather than fission, of atoms. Fusion is the force used in hydrogen bombs and the process that takes place in the heart of the sun. It utilizes the energy given off when atoms combine, rather than that released when they are torn apart. If it can be put to work in a reactor, fusion will permit us to use an inexhaustible source of energy—the deuterium in the sea.

The problems in the way of perfecting controlled fusion are immense. One of the greatest of them is how to contain the hot gases (plasmas), which will reach temperatures of around one hundred million degrees C.! Although progress is being made by researchers in several countries, no one can predict exactly when this ultimate power source will be available.

Perhaps, before then, science will find ways to turn to what now seems like an even farther out source of power—the radiant energy of the sun.

"In the long run," says Peter E. Glaser, past president of the Solar Energy Society, "only the sun offers a pollution-free electrical power source."

Many schemes have been worked out to use sunlight on a large scale. One of them is to lay out a grid of solar cells over the desert areas of the world—in New Mexico, Arizona and California in the United States and in the Sahara in Africa, for example. These solar cells would convert the heat of the sun directly into electricity. With efficient new transmission systems, such as the cryogenic tubes, it would be possible to supply the world's power needs from these sunny-area solar energy collectors. Another possibility is to cover wide areas with collecting mirrors that would develop heat to produce steam to operate generators.

Perhaps the most exciting development in solar power will come when we take power plants off our planet and put them out in space. This would be an engineering accomplishment of awesome proportions, but we already have the basic scientific knowledge that would make it possible. On an experimental scale, scientists have succeeded in transmitting power through the air by microwaves. Utilizing this ability, engineers have worked out huge systems of power-generating solar cells orbiting as satellites 22,300 miles above the equator. The orbital speed of these satellites would match that of the earth's rotation so that they would, in effect, always be in the same place above the earth.

If two satellites were orbited, 7,300 miles apart, one station would always be in sunlight. Via microwave, such a pair would be able to beam earthward a constant 20,000,000 kilowatts of power, which would be picked up by receiving stations in either hemisphere. This would be 12 times the power provided by Hoover Dam! With just a few such satellites, we could easily provide any conceivable amount of power the world could use.

Tracking Down Air Pollution

Until air pollution is completely cut off at its source, the pollution fighters will have to make increasing use of an important set of tools in their battle to make air breathable. These tools are the monitoring systems that detect the presence of pollutants. Consisting of instruments which sense components of the air and then report them to analyzing centers, they serve several purposes. They help scientists learn more about pollution; they help authorities spot the violators of regulations; they provide the warnings that alert authorities and citizens to the danger of a pollution crisis.

A typical monitoring system is the one in New York City. At various points in the city, electronic "sniffers" take in and analyze air samples. They translate their findings into electrical impulses which indicate the amount of a given pollutant present. These impulses are sent to a central computer in the Department of Air Resources headquarters in lower Manhattan. Other points are manned by observers who telephone in their readings. This information gives officials the data they need to determine whether to call a pollution alert that will shut down factories and take cars off the street.

Newly developed detectors are so sensitive that they can pinpoint the source of pollutants. The pioneering user of these sensors is the city of Rotterdam, the Netherlands. Automatic electronic sleuths are constantly on guard against situations such as the one that occurred one day in an industrial district. A factory which had run

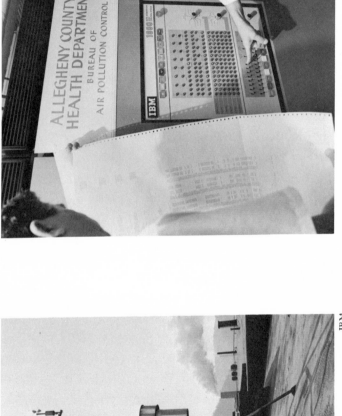

IBM

The data gathered by the sensors is fed into a central computer which analyzes data and indicates the need for pollution alerts.

IBM

This sensing device atop a roof in Pittsburgh is part of a monitoring system that provides a continuous flow of information about pollution levels in Allegheny County, Pennsylvania.

out of the low-sulfur fuel which antipollution laws required them to burn turned to using a high-sulfur oil for just one of the furnaces in the plant.

In a few moments a telephone in the office was ringing. "There's something wrong," an air pollution control official said, "with number-four chimney. It's sending up a lot of sulfur dioxide."

In some cities, mobile laboratories cruise the streets, zeroing in on such offenders and spotting dangerous pockets of air contamination. By the early '70s, all major cities in the United States and in most other countries will have complete monitoring systems.

Important though they are as a step toward protecting citizens from today's contaminated air, the city monitoring systems are only a start toward the larger ones that will be needed. A report of the National Air Pollution Control Administration states that "today's urban systems seldom extend beyond the city limits, leaving vast regions between cities unmonitored, or at best only partially monitored. It is in these regions that tomorrow's air pollution problems may be brewing. Also, with today's urban systems it is not possible to determine where the pollution came from, if it was produced inside or outside the city, or where air pollution goes after it leaves the city. If it cannot be monitored, it cannot be controlled."

Some planners visualize statewide and regional systems in which sensors spread out over large areas report their findings to centrally located computers. The ground instruments might be supplemented, or even made unnecessary, by instrument-equipped aircraft patrolling wide areas. This is a technique tried out over Washington, D.C., in 1969. Sensors aboard an airplane flying at 7,000 feet over the capital city successfully picked up ground-level readings showing the presence of sulfur dioxide.

The airborne sensors were able not only to determine the amounts of this substance, but also to indicate just where it was coming from. The discovery was made that not all of it was originating in the city itself, as many suburbanites in communities surrounding Washington had believed. It was true that 100 tons of sulfur dioxide was being carried out of the city every hour. However, 65 tons an hour was drifting into the city from Arlington County, Virginia.

The findings were valuable, but the experiment pointed up the limitations of using airplanes to spot sources of pollution. Low-flying aircraft are, of course, prohibited over certain parts of the city. Many other metropolitan areas have the same restrictions. The difficulty of arranging for enough flights over urban areas congested with air traffic is so difficult that scientists don't hold out much hope for the use of aircraft for pollution monitoring.

There is another promising tool that could solve the problem of large-scale continuous monitoring.

"If air pollution could be remotely monitored from an aircraft, then why not from a satellite?" asks Dr. Frederick F. Gorschboth, an advisory engineer for IBM.

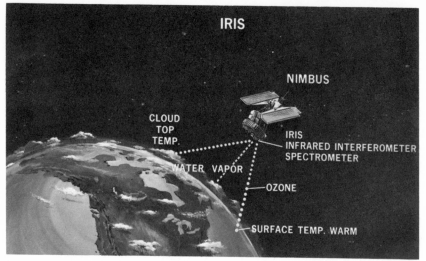

IRIS

NIMBUS

CLOUD
TOP
TEMP.

IRIS
INFRARED INTERFEROMETER
SPECTROMETER

WATER VAPOR

OZONE

SURFACE TEMP. WARM

NASA

Satellites in space will provide regional monitoring systems in the future. Instruments aboard the orbiting satellites can sense many atmospheric factors which influence pollution conditions.

"As a result of the Washington experiment," he reports,

IBM engineers have proposed a satellite survey from 600 miles out in space. Equipment, designed for use on the Nimbus weather satellite, would gather pollution data and transmit it to a computer system on the ground. The satellite data, correlated with data from the urban systems, could provide—for the first time—information on urban, regional, statewide and national pollution problems and trends.

Only large area surveys can address the problems of air pollution in areas like the megalopolis that has developed along the East Coast from the Carolinas to New York. A space-monitoring system can effectively track pollution plumes as they move across the cities of the eastern megalopolis—Washington, Boston, Baltimore, Philadelphia and New York.

Air pollution is a hierarchy of component problems—urban, regional and national. All are affected by the national weather picture. Among weather problems causing pollution are the large stagnating masses of air that slowly migrate across the nation. A space satellite is the only system capable of tracking such mammoth movements. A satellite can monitor the pollution level and distribution before the weather arrives in the area, while it is in the area and after it leaves the area.

By extending the satellite system, a national monitoring system could be developed that would answer national questions on pollution and, at the same time, monitor global trends and the effects of long-term pollution build-up in the earth's atmosphere. . . .

The space system could also check on natural pollutants emitted into the atmosphere, such as pollens, bacteria and marsh gases.

Air pollution is a total problem, one that calls for a total solution. Every force in technology's arsenal—urban systems, aircraft surveys and space satellites—must be employed in the attack on one of our nation's most urgent problems.

Clean Water for
Tomorrow's World

4

THE CHALLENGE of FRESHWATER POLLUTION

An astonishing sight greeted watchers along the Cuyahoga River in Ohio one day in 1969. An event long jokingly predicted had actually come to pass—the river was on fire! The oily debris that choked what was often called "the most polluted river in the United States" had ignited. Flames roared over the surface of the water, burning two railroad bridges and threatening structures along the shore.

This bizarre occurrence in Ohio dramatized the plight of America's ravaged rivers. The Cuyahoga may have had more inflammable pollutants in it than most rivers, but for sheer quantity of filth floating in its murky waters it had—and has—many rivals. All across the nation—and, indeed, in every part of the world—hundreds of rivers have become little better than open sewers. So, too, the

Great Lakes. Fresh water is in deep trouble in America, with few bodies of water escaping the spreading blight.

A look at the condition of one famous American river, the Potomac, and one of the Great Lakes, Lake Erie, gives a vivid picture of the freshwater pollution problem. Look first at "the Nation's River," which, in 1970, Secretary of the Interior Walter J. Hickel called "a shocking example of man's mistreatment of a natural resource—a national disgrace."

The Potomac runs for 385 miles before it reaches the District of Columbia. Up to that point, where, at Great Falls, it yields water supplies for Washington, D.C., it is relatively clear. But in the 114 miles between there and Chesapeake Bay the water of the Potomac changes to a filth-choked sewer that is even worse than it looks. A Federal Water Quality Administration report terms it "a severe threat to anyone coming in contact with it." "Sludge deposits have blanketed fish spawning grounds and destroyed the bottom aquatic life on which fish feed," the report continues. "Along the margins of the estuary, sludge deposits have released obnoxious odors when uncovered by the ebb tide. Floating sludge masses lifted by gases of decomposition add to other debris on the water's surface."

The slimy water has been described as having the appearance of "green latex paint." The 250,000,000 gallons a day of sewage that pours into it has been treated, but not enough. The result is that the equivalent of 80,000,000 gallons of totally untreated sewage is dumped into it every day. To be clean enough for swimming,

Pollution in the Potomac, one of the dirtiest rivers in America.
The water in it is often described as "thick green goo."

water should not contain more than 1,000 coliform organisms (intestinal bacteria) per one hundred milliliters. Coliform counts in the Potomac run as high as 4,000,000!

Turn to Lake Erie, the "lake that died,"and you see an even more dismal picture than that presented by the polluted Potomac. Into the once clear waters of this smallest of the Great Lakes, factories and cities dump 66 billion pounds of sediment every year. The sewage from a population of 3.8 million pours into it from the Detroit River alone. Just two of a score of steel plants add 137.5 *tons* of suspended solids in a single day. On its floor, 2,500 square miles are devoid of all life. A lake which provided a catch of a million pounds of fish annually just 20 years ago today yields hardly any. Sixty major beaches rimming the lake all show signs of pollu-

No swimming signs, sometimes ignored by bathers, appear on many beaches along Lake Erie, and on hundreds of other bodies of water that have become dangerously polluted.

tion; many of them have been closed. Along the shores, sludge-covered mud banks fester in what one reporter calls "a plastic ooze."

For a final touch, the waters of Lake Erie, after flowing down the Niagara River, create a brown foam at the foot of the famous falls, and visitors complain that the mist rising from the crashing water smells like sewage.

The blame for pollution, of which the Potomac River and Lake Erie are such frightening examples, cannot be placed on any one group in our society. Cities which fail to treat sewage properly, industries which pour out poisonous chemicals, Government officials who look the other way at violations of environmental laws and regulations, just plain citizens who casually toss trash into streams and lakes—all are guilty. And all must face the challenge of cleaning up the pollution mess. Fortunately, there is reason to believe that the challenge can be met. The problems are baffling, but promising solutions are already in sight. We can have clean lakes and rivers in tomorrow's world!

The Fertility Dilemma

"Here goes!"

Dr. David Woodbridge, of the Florida Institute of Technology, lifted a glass of clear water and drank it dry. What was so remarkable about that? Simply the fact that hours before he drank the water it had been raw sewage. The particular process that turned sewage into pure, odorless drinkable water called for the use of atomic energy. By bombarding the sewage with rays

Once pure rivers are turned into sewers by outpourings of sewage and industrial wastes.

Small streams as well as large are being damaged by pollutants.

from radioactive cobalt $^{-60}$, bacteria in it were destroyed.

Atomic irradiation is just one method that holds promise for solving the most troubling of water pollution problems—how to dispose of sewage without ruining rivers and lakes. Sewage dumped into the water does not simply contaminate it with harmful bacteria. It contributes to a process known as "eutrophication." Nutrients in sewage, chiefly from human wastes and detergents, become part of the ecological chain in a body of water and act as liquid fertilizer. This encourages the growth of green algae, and other microscopic plants and animals begin to thrive.

They live out their cycle and die, decomposing in the water. This not only puts a lot of decayed vegetative matter in the water but, in the process of decomposing, takes oxygen from it. When oxygen is removed, aquatic creatures die. Sometimes the growth of a particular organism is explosive. Touched off by the combination of sunlight, nutrients and organic matter, countless billions of the tiny plants or animals burst into what is called a "bloom." Many of these organisms which burst into such multitudinous life have a deadly effect on other creatures, producing toxins that paralyze respiratory organs.

The evil effects of eutrophication do not stop there. Dead plants, animals and fish settle on the bottom of the lake or slow-moving river, especially behind dams, forming thick mats of decaying matter. Slimy material clusters along shorelines, where it creates sickening odors.

The process of eutrophication is one that occurs in nature, especially in lakes, tidal estuaries and some very sluggish rivers. Nutrients washed from soil gradually increase plant growth. Eventually, the vegetation will turn a lake into a marsh. By adding nutritive wastes, man has brought about a fantastic speed-up, compressing centuries into decades.

Scientists use a device called a Secchi Disk to measure the amount of plant cells present in waste. This consists of a white disk that is lowered into the water on a calibrated line. The distance it can be seen through the water is an indication of how much its clarity is affected by organisms. In one badly eutrophicated lake in Maine, the water is so murky that the disk cannot be seen at a distance greater than two inches. In a clear lake it is visible through as much as 45 feet of water!

No wonder scientists believe that getting the nutrients

Eutrophication in an Ohio lake is studied by scientists. The monitoring machine through which the water is fed reveals basic information about the effects of nutrients on the water.

Dead algae, product of a dying lake, pile up on a once-clean beach.

out of sewage is an urgent problem. They hope it can be accomplished by processes that will also get out other pollutants; but, unfortunately, as most sewage is being treated today, this double requirement is not met.

There is nothing very new about the standard sewage treatment plants in use in most cities. Similar plants have been in existence for more than a hundred years, using the same methods. First, in what is called "primary" treatment, the sewage is passed through screens which catch large objects. Then it goes through a settling tank, where the water stands for a time, permitting some heavy substances to sink to the bottom, lighter ones to float to the top. The layer of water in between is then drained off and chlorinated to kill bacteria. This cleaned-up water is disposed of by releasing it into rivers and lakes. The solid sludge left behind is dried and used as fertilizer or landfill, or it may be burned.

This treatment removes only 35 per cent of pollutants, and the cost of a plant that carries the process this far works out to $35 a person. In other words, a city of one million must spend $35,000,000 to achieve a minimum treatment. Obviously, water with only 35 per cent of its pollutants removed should not be dumped into any stream, but, unfortunately, a majority of municipal sewage systems do just that.

If the sewage is put through this process more times, and more time is allowed in the settling tanks, a much bigger percentage of pollutants can be removed. Many plants are capable of 90 per cent success. The cost of building such plants goes up proportionately. A plant

These immense water purification ponds enable a paper mill to use water over and over again.

capable of removing 90 per cent of pollutants costs about $100 per person served. Thus, such a plant for a city of one million people will cost $100,000,000. This calls for the enormous bond issues which voters in many cities have been asked to vote for, and accounts for the fact that the total cost of providing adequate sewage disposal systems for all U.S. cities is put as high as $30 billion.

While these well-established methods work reasonably well, researchers hope for a breakthrough that will make sewage disposal both safer and cheaper. They would like a system so perfect that it will permit the reuse of water, cutting the drain on our water resources and, at the same time, reducing the load on rivers and lakes.

One such possible breakthrough is atomic irradiation, which is so effective that it produces pure, drinkable water, as Dr. Woodbridge demonstrated. In the pilot operation the first nuclear sewage plant in the world, set up at Fisheating Creek Campground, near Lake Okeechobee in Florida, sewage goes through the usual primary filtering process. Then the effluent is passed under the radioactive rays which emanate from a capsule of cobalt $^{-60}$.

This burst of radioactivity not only kills disease-causing bacteria and viruses but also breaks up harmful chemicals, such as DDT. Most important of all, in the opinion of some ecologists, it acts on the phosphates that play an important part in fertilizing waters and causing eutrophication.

The radioactivity which accomplishes this does not remain in the water. If it works out as scientists at the University Center for Pollution Research at Florida Institute of Technology hope, this system could wipe out water pollution by sewage at half the cost of conventional methods.

Researchers are exploring many other promising ways of purifying and disposing of sewage. One broad area of research is aimed at finding new kinds of filters that will screen out tiny units of matter. Some are based on processes developed to take the salt out of salt water. Other systems substitute chemical actions for the bacterial action now used in breaking down solids. Eventually, many environmental experts believe, all present methods can be done away with. When fusion power is developed, at some unpredictable time in the future, all wastes can be simply vaporized in fusion furnaces that will reduce them to basic elements.

Water once heavily polluted can emerge sparkling and clean
from processing plants.

Environmental scientists are hopeful that they can take a tremendous burden off sewage disposal plants and go a long way toward conquering eutrophication without any new system at all. They propose to begin in the kitchens and laundry rooms of America. The enemy they're tackling is the phosphate-laden detergent, which has been identified as the source of much of the fertility that has created pollution. In a single year, over four billion pounds of this highly efficient cleaning agent is used in the United States alone. Half of that poundage consists of phosphates, which act as fertilizers to plant life in waters into which they are dumped. Sewage treatment removes some of the phosphates, but most of them are poured into the streams and lakes.

Is there any way to take the phosphates out of detergents? Many manufacturers have protested that there isn't, since phosphates are the chemicals that give detergents their cleaning power. Removing them, said a spokesman for the Soap and Detergent Manufacturers Association, would "set back health, cleanliness and sanitation standards many years."

Many scientists, however, are sure that a substitute for the phosphates can be found, even though the chemical problem is not a simple one. There is always the lurking danger that a new chemical will, like the phosphates, turn out to have unexpected ill effects. Putting two billion pounds of any unknown substance into the environment is a worrisome prospect which Harvard pathologist Samuel Epstein terms "playing chemical roulette."

One substance that seemed to work turned out to have a corrosive effect on plumbing. Another, on which a major soap company is reported to have spent millions of dollars in research and over a hundred million in production facilities, worries medical authorities because when it is added to water it reacts with industrial pollutants, such as arsenic, to create compounds which, if they got into drinking water, could cause cancer.

"It's quite a choice," said one worried pollution control official. "Either we turn our lakes into swamps or the water we drink gets poisoned."

In spite of the problems, so many crash research programs are under way that some of them are bound to succeed. In fact, a few nonphosphate detergents had already appeared on the market in the early '70s.

The Killer Chemicals

When Norwald Fimreite, a graduate student at the University of Western Ontario, began studying the fish in Lake St. Clair, near Detroit, he had no idea he was going to make a discovery that would shock the governments of the United States and Canada and alert the world to a frightening pollution menace. Probably others would have made the same discovery he did; but, ecologists ask, what if they had made it years later instead of in 1970 as did this alert student? Possibly human lives would have been lost, along with the destruction of billlions of fish and other forms of marine life.

In his native Norway, Fimreite had studied an obscure phenomenon—the effects of mercury on birds and other wildlife. When he came to Canada to work for his Ph.D. in zoology, he decided he would pursue this interest further. In Norway, he had found evidence that some wild animals stored mercury in their systems. Predatory animals had more than others did. In other words, predatory animals, which eat other animals, accumulate all the mercury found in the systems of their prey.

Fimreite decided that the pickerel was a good subject for his studies. A predatory fish, feeding on many other kinds of fish, it should have higher concentrations of mercury than other species. As he started catching and analyzing fish in Lake St. Clair, he found that this was the case, all right. What jolted the young zoologist was the quantity of mercury. It was fantastically high—so high that he wondered if he could possibly be right. Yet, as he dissected fish after fish, he came to the stunning conclusion that, if anything, the quantities were even greater than he had at first thought. Not only the pickerel but other fishes too were loaded with mercury.

Now what is so terrible about mercury? Simply that it is one of the most toxic substances known to man. If it gets into the human body, it attacks the central nervous system. A form of the chemical, methyl mercury, tends to accumulate in the brain cells, producing a variety of disastrous results. An old expression, "mad as a hatter," indicates one of these results. At one time, mercury was used in making felt hats. Workers breathing its fumes literally went mad, as the poison affected their brains.

Other symptoms of mercury poisoning include an inability to control muscles; impaired speech, vision and hearing; and severe emotional disturbances. It has been determined that when a pregnant woman eats mercury-contaminated food, the poison accumulates in the nervous system of the fetus and can cause mental retardation or cerebral palsy. There have been outbreaks of mercury poisoning in the United States, Japan and other countries.

Knowledge of what mercury's effects could be was what alarmed Fimreite. Fish in Lake St. Clair were heavily contaminated with mercury—and people were eating them. It hardly seemed possible that no one had observed this danger before, but the zoology student hurried to tell Canadian officials what he had discovered. The scientists were duly shocked and promptly issued an order banning fishing in the lake. Within hours, U.S. officials issued a similar order for their portion of the lake. The U.S. Food and Drug Administration rushed to make tests, not only on fish in Lake St. Clair but in Lake Erie as well. The Federal Water Quality Administration began tests of fish in major rivers.

What they found, as many agencies pushed crash programs to investigate mercury pollution, was that a dangerous pollutant had somehow escaped attention. In the flurry of investigation, it was discovered that the widespread use of mercury in many industrial processes—the making of pulp and paper, plastics and chemicals—was resulting in the release of an estimated 1.2 million pounds of it into the waters of the United States and Canada each year. Dangerous amounts of it were found in 14 eastern rivers. Late in 1970, it was discovered that the oceans had been contaminated. Tuna and swordfish had absorbed such large amounts of the substance that the Food and Drug Administration ordered quantities of canned fish off the market.

While injury to people was not indicated, the potential was there. Only carelessness and ignorance of the dangers ever let loose vast quantities of this poisonous substance. Now, with heavy penalties imposed on any industry that lets any of it escape, further contamination of water by mercury should stop, although the problem of dealing with the quantities of it already in the water is a formidable one.

The list of industrial pollutants which are known to be fouling the fresh waters of the nation is a long one. Each industry develops a special class of contaminants which somehow end up in the streams and lakes. Many of them come from the chemical industry itself, which rates as the fastest growing of all industries. It is made up of some 13,500 plants, turning out no less than 10,000 different kinds of chemicals.

The danger of permitting chemicals to get into water at all lies in the fact that their consequences may be unknown. One chemical plant, for example, dumped 30 pounds of a new pesticide into a river. It was thought to be harmless, but it killed over 50,000 fish. The experience with mercury has resulted in a much closer look at such poisons as arsenic, chromium and selenium, which were not previously thought of as dangerous, but which are showing up in fish in increasing quantities. A typical example of chemical plant pollution occurred on the Kanawha River in West Virginia, into which one fac-

The purified waste water from the oil refinery in the background is clean enough to make these birds feel at home in the marsh fed by this industrial effluent.

tory poured 300,000,000 gallons of polluted water a day.

In terms of sheer quantity, the worst industrial offender is the paper industry. Dr. Roger Revelle, of Harvard's School of Public Health, estimates that the organic material it puts into the waters of the United States is greater in amount than all the nation's sewage. One paper plant on Lake Champlain in New York, for example, dumped 28,400 pounds of solids into the lake every day. Near the plant, they had built up a delta of chemicals 12 feet deep. Another plant had deposited so much waste on the floor of a lake that efforts to dredge it away met with failure. The dredge could not cut down through the solid mass of pollutants.

Many other industries are, by their nature, dirty. The quantity of pollutants given off by the metal industries is illustrated by a typical large steel plant which disposes of organic wastes equivalent in amount to the sewage from a city of 300,000 people. In addition to these substances, its waste water contains quantities of ammonia, phenol, cyanide and many other chemicals.

A single textile plant may pour out a score of different wastes such as dyes, fixing agents, resins, starches and acids. Altogether, 90 different chemicals have been found in textile wastes. Oil refineries, which are among the largest users of water, emit vast quantities of organic substances that complicate the eutrophication problem caused by sewage.

Formidable as the task of stemming this tide of industrial pollutants may be, the prospects of success are bright. No breakthrough in technology is called for to keep damaging chemicals out of rivers and lakes. The processes for treating water are well established, and many industries are applying them. The instances of complete success are numerous.

A West Coast paper mill near Sacramento turns out water so clean that salmon swim right outside the waste outlets. A chemical factory in West Virginia removes pollutants so completely that people enjoy boating, fishing and swimming on the river below the plant. Birds and other wildlife thrive in a once polluted lagoon fed by waste water from a refinery. These successes point the way to a future in which industry will no longer damage the vast quantities of water which it must use to make possible the technologically advanced world of today—and tomorrow.

The Heat Hazard

Every year 50 trillion gallons of water are used by power plants and factories to carry away not waste substances but heat. Even though nothing tangible has been added to this water, it presents a troubling pollution problem today, and will present a much greater one tomorrow. As power needs increase, so does the use of water for cooling. It is estimated that the amount needed by power plants—both fossil fuel and nuclear—will increase nine times by the year 2000. "By that time," says one power industry report, "at least 50 per cent of all the waters flowing across the surface of the United States will have to be used to cool power plant condensers."

Not only power plants but many industries, and even public buildings, spew out hot water. The heat taken from the air by air conditioners in the giant World Trade Center in lower Manhattan actually raises the temperature of the Hudson River 10 degrees near the outlet where the water used for cooling feeds into the river. Water from refineries has been known to raise the temperature of a stretch of river to 120° F.

Why is heat regarded as a pollutant? Why isn't it all right to raise the temperature of water, if no contaminants are added to it? There are many reasons, but the main one is its effect on marine life.

"Temperature is very important in any environment," says Dr. Willis S. Osborn, of the Atomic Energy Commission. "When you raise the temperature anywhere, you can't help but drive it over the level where at least some

The round structure at the right is a cooling tower—an important tool for curbing thermal water pollution.

of the myriad organisms in the system cannot survive."

If a river is heated to 90° F., some fish die, some become unconscious and, zoologists say, all are affected. Higher temperatures produce higher death rates. Death may be caused directly by overheating, or it may result from asphyxiation. Since dissolved oxygen is necessary for marine life, any drop in the amount of it present in the water can endanger fish. Hot water has less dissolved oxygen. The hotter it is, the greater the drop in oxygen.

If this effect of heat is combined with the effects of pollution, which has already reduced oxygen, the results can be catastrophic. Fish, which can swim away from overheated areas, are more fortunate than creatures which are not so mobile. Along one river in New England, for example, it was found that at a point where a coal-burning power plant discharged its cooling water, some 40,000 blue crabs had died.

Curiously enough, raising the temperature of water can sometimes have the effect of *increasing* the amount of oxygen, with equally deadly results on fish. The heat encourages the growth of algae, much as do the nutrients in sewage, and an algae "bloom" can result. The billions of tiny plants that have burst into life, when acted upon by sunlight, release so much dissolved oxygen that the fish die of what is called "supersaturation."

Fortunately, there is no need to stand by and watch heat kill off the living creatures of streams, lakes and bays. There are many solutions to this growing problem. Obviously, a basic one is to cool the water to levels closer to the natural temperature of the body of water from which it is taken and to which it is to be returned.

This can be done quite simply by setting up cooling ponds—artificial lakes which receive the hot water and retain it long enough for it to cool off. Scientists have suggested that in some climates the water could be cooled faster if swamp plants or tropical trees like mangroves were planted around the ponds. The plants would give off water through normal transpiration, setting up an evaporative cooling system that would lower the temperature of the water.

Another way to take the heat out of water is to use a cooling tower, really a huge radiator. It may be hundreds of feet high, like a 437-foot giant built by the TVA. In such a tower, water is circulated through a network of pipes and forced out through thousands of sprinkler heads inside the tower, where it then falls into a collection basin at the bottom. It is pumped through the sprinklers over and over again and each time it falls it loses heat in the cooling draft that continually blows upwards inside the tower. Only 2 per cent of the water is lost through evaporation.

But why waste all that heat? engineers ask. The hot water could be piped to heat not only the factory or power plant but also buildings and homes some distance away. Agriculturalists see waste heat from power plants as a way to warm the soil and extend the growing season. At the Hanford nuclear plant in Richland, Washington, this has already been tried. Hot water moving through pipes buried in the soil makes seeds germinate rapidly and speeds up the growth of plants.

A long-range plan to meet America's power shortage

can also help beat the heat problems. An increasingly large part of the nation's energy requirements will come from nuclear power plants. Engineers suggest building "power islands" in the sea. Some miles offshore, in water as much as several hundred feet deep, earth could be dredged and pumped up from the sea bottom or hauled by barge from land. Possibly some of the landfill could be made with garbage, thereby helping solve our solid waste disposal problem. On this man-made island, nuclear power plants would be built. They could be used not only to produce power but also to desalt sea water, extract nitrogen from the air for use as fertilizer and possibly perform other industrial tasks. Underwater cables would carry the electricity to land, where it could be fed into the power grids.

Ecologists believe that water used for cooling in power plants at sea could safely be returned to the water surrounding them, only slightly raising its temperature, not enough to have any injurious effects on marine life.

5

PROTECTING the WORLD'S OCEANS

When Thor Heyerdahl set out to cross the Atlantic in a papyrus boat to prove that the ancient Egyptians could have made such a voyage, he saw something that no early-day mariner could have witnessed.

In his radio message of June 13, 1970, Heyerdahl said, "During 27 days of sailing so far, oil lumps in varying sizes have been observed uninterruptedly every day. . . . At least a continuous stretch of 1,400 miles of the open Atlantic is polluted by floating lumps of solidified asphalt-like oil. . . .There have been days when it has been impossible to fix the eyes on any part of the sea without seeing pollution floating in individual bits and clusters."

Of course, many others had reported that man-made pollution had invaded the farthest reaches of the sea, but coming from the noted anthropologist the information

106

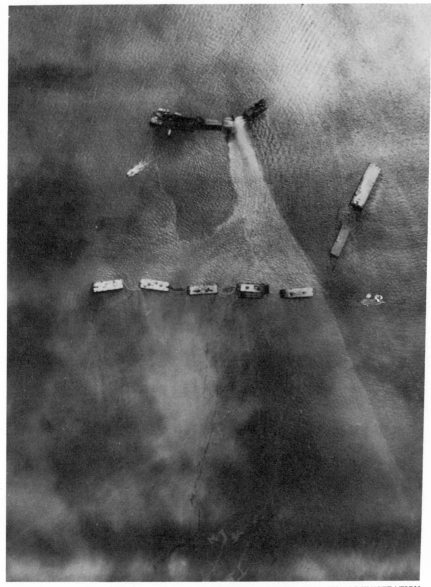

FEDERAL WATER QUALITY ADMINISTRATION

Oil spill! This infrared photo shows oil pouring out from the burned platform off Louisiana after the fires were put out on March 10, 1970. The line of barges and booms were used to try to stop the spread of the oil.

seemed particularly dramatic. As it made front-page stories in newspapers all over the world, it conveyed to millions of people the message that pollution was not confined to inland rivers and lakes and areas close to ocean shores. The seas, long looked upon as a reservoir that could serve as a bottomless dumping ground for any amount of civilization's refuse, were turning out to be, in the words of writer Wesley Marx, "the frail oceans."

The truth is that the oceans, boundless as they seem, are being damaged by the spreading blight of pollution, just as are the fresh waters. Not only are ships spewing out ugly blots of oil, but an incredible range of pollutants are choking the seas. Man is deliberately using them as a repository for sewage, garbage, junked automobiles, radioactive waste, surplus military weapons, such as nerve gas, and corrosive industrial chemicals. By accident, other pollutants are constantly being added, as offshore oil wells run wild, dirty rivers run off into the sea and tankers go aground.

The sea is not uniformly polluted by the 48,000,000 tons of material dumped into it each year. Many areas close to shore are particularly blighted. For example, the area off New York harbor, where sludge and other wastes have been dumped for years, is devoid of sea life. Over a wide area, the oxygen in the water, which has to be at a level of at least 2.5 parts per million to sustain life, has been cut to less than 1 part per million. Some counts of pollutants run a murderous 151 parts per million of lead, 60 of copper and 150 of DDT. There are a number of other dumping areas along the East Coast and the Gulf of Mexico where similar conditions exist.

The Oil Spill Menace

The need for oil has sent geologists into the far reaches of the globe in a hunt for the vital "black gold." In deserts, jungles and bleak Arctic tundra, they have found vast new deposits, but the most promising supply of all is at our own doorstep—in the shallow waters of the seas off our shores. The development of huge platforms and underwater drilling techniques have made it possible to tap vast treasure troves of oil that does not have to be transported thousands of miles to reach our refineries. Operating in federally controlled waters, beyond the 3-mile limit, there are more than 3,000 active wells already, with the prospect that thousands more will be added. Most people do not propose that we abandon offshore oil wells, but the need to exploit this underwater petroleum bonanza confronts us with unexpected new water pollution problems.

The most frightening example of what can happen was demonstrated in Santa Barbara, California. It began in January, 1969, when a geyser of mud came shooting up from a well which was being drilled. In a moment a black mist enveloped the platform. In spite of the ear-splitting roar, the choking gases and the fear of fire, the workers stuck to their posts, dropping the drill string back into the well. There they used hydraulic rams to force it into the well head, closing it off. The flow of oil stopped.

As many as a dozen wells can be drilled from giant platforms such as this. Oil from offshore deposits is needed, but oil spills are a danger which engineers are working hard to avoid in the future.

Then, 200 yards off the platform, the surface of the water began to boil, in a froth of natural gas and oil. As it crept toward the platform, the workers took to boats. The Santa Barbara oil spill was on its way to fame.

When worried oil company engineers and geologists took stock, they determined that the oil had actually forced its way through cracks in the earth. Later, a U.S. Geological Survey expert, Dr. Thane McCulloch, made a dive on the site and proved that this was indeed the case. "On the sea floor oil issued as streams from pinpoint and larger openings in siltstone and soft sediment alike," he announced.

Where was the oil coming from? The men who tried to stop the flow made the discovery that the well, which went down to a depth of over 3,400 feet, had no casing (pipe) for most of its depth. In fact, the casing extended down only 239 feet. Unrestrained by pipes, the oil, under tremendous pressure, had broken out of the drill hole and was escaping through weak places and cracks in the earth. It was determined that these flows of oil were occurring over a 50-acre area.

In ten days, by using 13,000 barrels of sealant, workers managed to seal off the well itself, though oil continued to boil up through the fissures. For the first three days, an offshore wind kept the growing slick, building up at the rate of 5,000 gallons a day, away from Santa Barbara. But on the fourth day, the wind changed, and the gleaming white sands of the city's famous beaches began to turn black. With each incoming tide, the dark rim crept over more sand. Boats in the harbor were coated. Oil marks extended ten feet high on seawalls. By the eighth day the slick had spread along 100 miles of shore and covered 660 square miles of water in the Santa Barbara Channel.

The battle to control the oil flow went on for more that three months, and even at the end of that time there was still some seepage of oil through the fissures. The beaches were eventually cleared up by oil company workers using various methods, such as soaking up the oil with straw. Thousands of oil-soaked seabirds, whose greasy feathers kept them from flying, were saved by volunteers who washed them clean.

The fear that the happening at Santa Barbara could occur elsewhere was firmly planted in the minds of millions. The Government, the oil companies and aroused conservationists vowed that it would not happen again. However, it did—in the great oil spill off Louisiana a little over a year later.

Eleven miles offshore stood an enormous platform, one of the largest ever built. From this mile-long structure, 12 oil wells had been drilled. There had been no hint of trouble until the morning of February 10, 1970, when, suddenly, everything went wrong. A gas well blew out of control, hurling gas, oil and tools skyward with enormous force. Shortly, another well blew, and then another, until eight were out of control. Then, while workers scrambled for their lives, the platform burst into flame.

An aerial and marine fleet of professional firefighters moved in, with ships, helicopters and dynamite. It was March 10, exactly a month after it all started, before the last flames were finally choked off. And then a new hazard arose. No longer consumed by the raging flames, 42,000 gallons of crude oil spilled out every day into the Gulf. While hundreds of workers, with dynamite, drilling mud and sheets of lead, fought to seal off the wells, the ugly black slick of oil spread over hundreds of square miles.

The worry haunting ecologists was that there might be a change in the wind direction. Fortunately, at that time of year, the wind usually blows offshore. Thus the oil was pushed toward the sea. Had the spill occurred in the summer, with the wind coming from the water, it would have meant catastrophe for the teeming wildlife in the marshes and estuaries of the Louisiana shore.

These two shocking experiences, which so vividly

demonstrated the destructive potential of oil spills, were costly, but their magnitude and drama made them a valuable object lesson for industry, government and science. Investigations showed that the disasters need not have happened. The oil companies, in some cases with Government approval, had not been using the safety methods that had been developed to prevent exactly this kind of mishap. Safety valves that will shut off the flow of oil in an emergency, more careful drilling, casings extended to greater depths and many other techniques can make offshore drilling safe.

The oil spills from offshore wells, however, are only part of the petroleum pollution problem. Actually, tankers present a much greater menace. In a single year there were 950 spills resulting from accidents to tankers. These accidents included that of the *Torrey Canyon,* which went aground off the coast of England, spilling 30,000,000 gallons of crude oil, damaging miles of beaches and killing 200,000 seabirds; the *Ocean Eagle,* which went aground near San Juan, Puerto Rico, polluting the harbor; and the *Mary Z. Whalen,* which went aground off Rockaway Point, New York, fouling 20 beaches.

In addition to oil spilled by actual groundings, vast amounts of it are poured into the seas from tankers which flush their tanks at sea. Estimates of oil from this source run as high as 1,000,000 tons a year. Some ecologists calculate that oil entering the sea from all sources—shipwrecks, flushing and pollution of rivers flowing into the sea—could run as high as 50,000,000 tons in a year!

Fortunately, as in the case of the offshore wells, no

Tankers are getting bigger, and the danger of their contaminating beaches grows accordingly. Many go aground each year.

breakthrough in technology is required to stop the pollution by tankers. Tanks do not need to be flushed at sea. When oil does get away, as in a tanker shipwreck, there are a number of ways to keep it from becoming a massive spill. One way is to use emulsifiers, chemicals which, when sprayed on the oil, keep the drops of oil from joining together. Other chemicals can be used as solvents, to break up oil particles. The drawbacks to the use of chemicals for such purposes is their possible effect on marine life.

A promising approach is a newly invented machine which literally soaks up oil, sweeping it from the surface as it is pushed through the water by a small boat. A conveyor delivers the oil to tanks aboard the boat. Had it been available at the time of the *Torrey Canyon* shipwreck or the Santa Barbara episode, it would have saved the beaches from the black disaster which befell them. Such a machine can also be used to clean up harbors.

The Deadly Wastes

Until recently the sea was looked upon as a handy place to dump any kind of a substance too dangerous to dispose of elsewhere. It took a dramatic and frightening threat to convince many Americans that the ocean can no longer be used as a catch-all for deadly wastes.

ARMY TO DUMP NERVE GAS IN OCEAN, read the headlines that introduced the public to what came to be known as The Case of the 400 Coffins. In an earlier period, the U.S. Army had stockpiled 12,500 M-55 rockets which were tipped with a deadly nerve gas. Upon ex-

STANDARD OIL COMPANY, N.J.

Specially equipped vessels can prevent the spread of oil spills by breaking up the oil film. Other ships can skim it from the water before it reaches shore.

An oil vacuum cleaner which can clean up oil film from harbors and beaches. Use of such devices could have kept oil from reaching the beaches in the Santa Barbara disaster.

U.S. NAVY

plosion these fearsome weapons were designed to spray the gas, paralyzing anybody within range.

The military had decided not to use the hellish devices. So—what could be done with them? Military experts figured that the first thing to do was to seal them in concrete, which they proceeded to do, packing them in coffinlike concrete boxes. Next, what to do with the coffins? Why, dump them in the sea, of course.

The Army picked a spot near Bermuda where the water had a depth of 16,000 feet. When this plan was announced, a storm of protest arose. Environmental scientists argued that there was no guarantee that the sea water would not eat through the concrete, eventually releasing the nerve gas. The British Government expressed its concern at having the boxes dropped in waters so close to Bermuda and the Bahamas. U.N. Secretary U Thant was opposed to the scheme.

The affair turned out badly for concerned environmentalists because it was eventually decided that there was no workable alternative to burial at sea. The Army was condemned for lack of research into ways of disposing of such substances as the nerve gas, and the Atomic Energy Commission also came under criticism because it was reluctant to destroy the troublesome coffins, gas and all, in an underground nuclear explosion. The containers were duly transported from arsenals in Arkansas and Kentucky, and deposited in deep water some 300 miles from Cape Kennedy. Some ecologists still fear that someday the nerve gas will be released; others are sure it won't.

Even though the particular battle was lost, the environmentalists did win a long-range victory. Many scientists have gone to work on the previously neglected problem of disposing of dangerous wastes. Their research programs will reveal the extent of the dangers, and lead to alternatives, such as nuclear destruction, that can save the world from some future ecological catastrophe.

The uproar about the nerve gas focused attention on what many scientists believe creates a far greater pollution menace—the dumping of radioactive wastes at sea. As the number of atomic power plants grows, so do the "hot" waste products that must be disposed of. Fuels which have been expended are still radioactive. Atomic scientists have tried sealing them in containers and burying them deep underground. However, it has been simpler to dump the containers at sea.

At first, this procedure seemed safe, since the wastes were carried to the most remote parts of the Atlantic. However, later investigations showed that some of the containers had burst, crumpling inward under the pressure of the sea. This is something the scientists had not thought would happen, and there is much concern about it among nuclear authorities.

"Every living thing on and under the sea is being poisoned with radioactive wastes," says Dr. Jerold M. Lowenstein, of the University of California Medical Center at San Francisco.

He is referring not only to the limited amount of radioactivity imparted by wastes disposed of at sea, but also to the far greater quantities coming directly from power stations, and from nuclear powered ships and submarines.

Are pollutants destroying marine life? Ecological studies such as the one being made by these scientists reveal the effects of pollution close to shore.

A study of the Irish sea near the British Winscale nuclear power station revealed that radioactivity has become so high that embyro fishes develop deformed backbones. Release of radioactivity from British and American power plants has been rigorously controlled, but, as many nations turn to nuclear power, ecologists fear that some nations imposing controls may be less strict.

In spite of the hazards radioactivity presents there is no international organization which can control dumping "hot" wastes in the sea. The International Atomic Energy Agency, a unit of the United Nations, has been suggested as a logical authority. However, many ecologists believe that a new international sea authority should be set up to deal not only with problems of radioactivity, but with any of the deadly wastes that may pollute the seven seas.

All the pollutants that enter all the rivers of the world eventually end up in the oceans. This infrared photograph shows the distribution of water from the Quinault River, in the state of Washington, as it enters the sea.

Ending the Insecticide Menace

The end of the ocean came late in the summer of 1979, and it came even more rapidly than the biologists had expected. There had been signs for more than a decade, commencing with the discovery in 1968 that DDT slows down photosynthesis in marine plant life. It was announced in a short paper in the technical journal, *Science*, but to ecologists it smacked of doomsday. They knew that all life in the sea depends on photosynthesis, the chemical process by which green plants bind the sun's energy and make it available to living things. And they knew that DDT and similar chlorinated hydrocarbons had polluted the entire surface of the earth, including the sea.

But that was only the first of many signs. There had been

the final gasp of the whaling industry in 1973, and the end of the Peruvian anchovy fishery in 1975. Indeed, a score of other fisheries had disappeared quietly from overexploitation and various eco-catastrophes by 1977. The term "eco-catastrophe" was coined by a California ecologist in 1969 to describe the most spectacular of man's attacks on the systems which sustain his life. He drew his inspiration from the Santa Barbara offshore oil disaster of that year, and from the news which spread among naturalists that virtually all of the Golden State's seashore bird life was doomed because of chlorinated hydrocarbon interference with its reproduction. Eco-catastrophes in the sea became increasingly common in the early 1970s. Mysterious "blooms" of previously rare microorganisms began to appear in offshore waters. Red tides —killer outbreaks of a minute single-celled plant—returned to the Florida Gulf coast and were sometimes accompanied by tides of other exotic hues.

It was clear by 1975 that the entire ecology of the ocean was changing. A few types of phytoplankton were becoming resistant to chlorinated hydrocarbons and were gaining the upper hand. Changes in the phytoplankton community led inevitably to changes in the community of zooplankton, the tiny animals which eat the phytoplankton. These changes were passed on up the chains of life in the ocean to the herring, plaice, cod and tuna. As the diversity of life in the ocean diminished, its stability also decreased.

Other changes had taken place by 1975. Most ocean fishes that returned to fresh water to breed, like the salmon, had become extinct, their breeding streams so damned up and polluted that their powerful homing instinct only resulted in suicide. Many fishes and shellfishes that bred in restricted areas along the coasts followed them as onshore pollution escalated.

By 1977 the annual yield of fish from the sea was down to 30 million metric tons, less than one half the per capita catch of a decade earlier. This helped malnutrition to escalate sharply in a world where an estimated 50 million people per year were already dying of starvation.

Everyone hopes that nothing like this grim "prophecy" by Dr. Paul Ehrlich, Professor of Biology at Stanford University, ever comes true. Yet the events he describes as future possibilities are well on their way toward reality in the early 1970s. The oceans are menaced by DDT and other insecticides. Their effects, so vividly described at the start of the '60s by Rachel Carson in her classic *Silent Spring*, may well result in more than catastrophic damage to sea life. Breathed in by livestock, wildlife, poultry and people, and contaminating the food they eat, insecticides, if their use continued to be widespread, could damage all life on this planet. However, some of the most disastrous and observable effects would occur in the oceans, in somewhat the manner Dr. Ehrlich has outlined. The ocean is the ultimate dumping ground for a high percentage of all air and water pollutants.

The battle against pollution by insecticides is one of the most hopeful areas in the struggle to clean up our environment. Scientists predict that within a short time we can completely end this form of pollution by simply

Researchers are working on a new approach to insecticides. Being tested here is a pesticide that is chemically changed to a harmless substance after it has done its work of destroying insects.

stopping the use of chemical insecticides. And let insects take over the world? Not at all. We will be able to destroy the harmful insects—which cause a $4 billion a year crop loss in the United States—but we won't do it with chemicals. Agricultural scientists have developed a host of weapons that will enable us to wage war on insects without causing an environmental backlash.

The list of harmless nonchemical weapons against insects starts with several forms of biological warfare. One system gets bugs to cooperate in their own destruction. Scientists at the U.S. Department of Agriculture research laboratories in Beltsville, Maryland, are using the ability of male insects to smell female insects as much as three miles away. The secret is a powerful sex attractant—different for each species of bug. It is this substance that the scientists are succeeding in using in place of DDT.

This is the way it worked out in the case of the gypsy moth, a species that devastates whole forests. A team of researchers, led by entomologist Dr. Martin Jacobson, first gathered half a million female moths. From them they succeeded in extracting exactly two drops of the chemical that attracts male moths. With this to go on, they managed to create a synthetic form of it, which they call "gyplure." They then designed an inexpensive trap, in the form of a small cardboard cup with a slanting lip at the opening. Baited with a touch of "gyplure" the trap became irresistibly attractive to male moths, which, after landing on the lip, were held fast by a sticky substance. Dropped by the thousands in forest areas, the traps have

Biological warfare replaces insecticides. This USDA plane is fighting pests that attack cotton plants. It drops such large numbers of sterile moths that mating between fertile moths seldom occurs. Thus fewer and fewer eggs turn into the damaging pink cotton bollworm.

stopped moth invasions in wide areas of New England and the Midwest.

An improved version that lets the trapped moth go has proved even more effective. Added to the sex lure in the trap was another substance which had the effect of sterilizing the male. That meant that females mating with the sterile male laid infertile eggs which did not hatch. Sterilizing traps have been developed for many species of bugs, but finding chemicals that stand up under exposure to the weather is a problem.

Scientists have found other ways to sterilize insects. One of them is to subject batches to nonlethal doses of atomic radiation. This can be accomplished simply by placing them in a chamber with a small amount of cobalt^{-50}. The results of releasing a large number of sterilized males in an area can be dramatic. In the early years of experimenting with this type of pest control, USDA scientists got a call from officials on the island of Curaçao, in the West Indies. A certain kind of fly was attacking goats on the island. Might the sterilized-fly scheme work? The entomologists at Beltsville shipped down such flies by the millions. Released in successive batches, they caused a drop in the size of each generation of flies. In less than four months, flies of that species were extinct on the island.

Another promising line of attack is to use bugs to fight bugs. USDA scientists are searching the world for harmless insects that act as predators on harmful species. The task to which they have set themselves calls for testing literally millions of types of bugs, but they have already achieved some remarkable results. A wasp imported from France, for instance, attacks certain beetles that damage trees.

Other entomologists are using viruses to kill bugs. This approach calls for isolating particular kinds of virus that can attack certain species. The process of finding such viruses is a slow, painstaking one, but more than a score have been discovered which can prove effective against some of the most destructive insects. Applied as a dust or spray, the viruses with a deadly effect on only one kind of bug could wipe out a whole species in any given area. The gravest problem for scientists in this kind of virus warfare is that they must prove first, beyond any doubt, that the virus will harm only its intended victim.

Another tool for destroying bugs without DDT is light. Certain wavelengths can be used to attract bugs to a

Clean water, clean beaches are one of the promises of tomor-row's world if we win the fight to protect the oceans from pollution.

source where ultraviolet rays can then kill them. This method, too, calls for much research to find the exact wavelength that will attract particular species, but the results have been rewarding. One light, found to attract a certain kind of gnat, proved so effective that a single trap caught no less than 85,000,000 gnats in a single night. When traps were used against the destructive corn borer, fields that required as many as ten dustings with ordinary pesticides were cleared by traps operating for a few nights.

With these and many other promising tools of destruction being researched, it seems that the day is coming soon when man will not have to use DDT to fight off his insect enemies. We can have lakes, rivers and seas that are no longer menaced by the chemical insecticides that have turned out to be a danger to our environment.

Water Resources for Tomorrow's World

6

WATER for a THIRSTY WORLD

Where will we get the water we need for a thirsty world?

This is a question we must answer, for even if we win the battle against water pollution, we will still face the problem of finding new sources of water for a world that needs more and more of it every year. In 1970, we were using 350 billion gallons a day in the United States. By 1980, estimates place the need at 600 billion gallons a day. Sometime before the year 2000, experts predict, the need will soar beyond a *trillion* gallons a day.

And these astronomical figures are for the United States alone. Almost all other countries will have to find sources that will increase their supplies of water by equal or greater amounts. Some of the developing countries, which are just beginning to expand and modernize their economies, will need as much as 1,000 per cent more.

Water for the homes and industries of Chicago flows through this giant pipe, part of the world's largest water purification plant. Every individual in a large modern city requires more than 200 gallons of water a day for domestic use alone.

A drought in the early '60s gave people who lived in the Northeastern part of the United States a frightening glimpse of what a world without enough water would be like. After four years, in which the equivalent of a full year's rainfall was lost, the drought reached a climax in 1965. In New York, swimming pools and fountains were shut down. Auto washing and lawn sprinkling were forbidden. Industries began to slow production. In the countryside, fields turned brown. Crops were failing in parts of New Jersey and upstate New York. New York City officials looked with alarm at the dwindling supplies in the city's reservoirs. With a capacity of 476.5 billion gallons, their contents had dropped to a dangerously low 240 billion gallons.

Desperate water system officials found themselves unable to turn to emergency sources such as the Hudson River because the water in it was so heavily polluted that it could not be used for any domestic or industrial purpose. The Delaware, which had always been an important source of water, was severely damaged by the drought. There was not enough water in it to dilute the wastes that were allowed to pour into it, and organic and chemical pollutants were increasing rapidly. To make matters worse, tidal action carried salt water far upstream in the Delaware and other shrinking, polluted rivers. When many cities turned to wells, water tables fell, causing salt water to move in underground, contaminating wells all along the Atlantic coast.

Fortunately, the rains came. A normal amount of rainfall in the following few years brought the supplies of water back to safe levels. However, many people, including public officials, who had never given much thought to water supplies before, were shaken by the event. "What would have happened the next year, if there had been no replenishing rains?" they asked.

A U.S. Geological Survey report sounded a warning: "The critical water shortages in the Northeast were a forecast of hardships that may arise in the future. A prolonged dry period in the Northeast, or in any other part of the United States, could have a more serious impact on a population significantly larger than it is today. With ever increasing demands upon available supplies, the results could be catastrophic."

Even without the occurrence of drought conditions, we face disaster if we do not develop more sources of water supply. If you're an inhabitant of an American city you use an average of 200 gallons every day just to meet domestic needs—taking showers, flushing toilets, washing clothes and dishes, watering lawns. That means that a family of five uses 1,000 gallons of water a day, just in the home.

And home use is a small part of the water demands of the nation. Industry uses prodigious quantities of water for cooling, washing, flushing and various chemical processes. It takes 44,000 gallons of water to build a single automobile, 365,000 gallons of water to make a ton of rayon and 1,000,000 gallons of water to make 1,000 gallons of gasoline. Agriculture requires a torrent of water—75 gallons to produce one ear of corn and 23,000 gallons to produce one pound of meat.

Agriculture . . . and . . .

. . . industry require vast quantities of water.

There is no way to greatly reduce these water demands, which, of course, keep going up in proportion to population gains and to the amount of goods we consume and food we eat. There is, therefore, only one answer: we must find new sources of water.

Is there enough water on our planet to meet the needs of tomorrow? Fortunately, say the hydrologists, there is plenty. What we must do is find ways to put it to use. And that will take some doing, for the world's water supply is not set up for human convenience. Look at the sources of the world's water, as outlined by the U.S. Geological Survey:

Location	Water Volume (in cubic miles)	Percentage of Total Water
Fresh water lakes	30,000	.009
Saline lakes and inland seas	25,000	.008
Rivers and streams	300	.0001
Soil moisture and near-the-surface ground water	16,000	.005
Ground water (within depth of half a mile)	1,000,000	.31
Ground water (deep lying)	1,000,000	.31
Icecaps and glaciers	7,000,000	2.15
Atmosphere (at sea level)	3,100	.0001
Oceans	317,000,000	97.2

As you can readily see, this distribution of water poses two basic challenges which we will have to meet in solving water supply problems of the future. Since fresh water represents only 2.8 per cent of the total water supply in the world, we will have to find better ways to use this limited amount of fresh water. We will have to tap sources we have ignored in the past, and we will have to find ways to conserve water.

The other broad challenge is that most of the world's water—a staggering 97.2 per cent of it—is in the oceans. We must transform some of this vast supply from salt water to fresh. Both challenges can be met, not by any one means but by many.

Reusing Water

"We've got to stop throwing water away!"

This is the point of a Federal Water Quality Administration report of 1970. Water experts have concluded that the most promising way to start the task of providing more water is to reuse what we already have. In other words, recycle sewage and industrial waste water, using it again and again—and again.

". . . Some 60 to 90 per cent of the water delivered to a city is returned to waste discharge. If treated to the conventional secondary level, this waste contains, usually, less than 1/10 of 1 per cent of impurities, and advanced waste treatment can make it completely suitable for a wide range of uses," says the FWQA report.

Pioneering ventures have already demonstrated the workability of water reuse. The first city in the world to make wide use of treated sewage effluent is Windhoek, the capital of South-West Africa. When this city of 36,000 was faced with a desperate water shortage in the late '60s, officials decided that overburdened wells could not keep up with the demands. Local citizens expressed distaste for the idea of recycling, but a water shortage looked even worse. The treated water from sewage now provides one-third of the city's water supply. Taste tests indicate that no one can tell the source of the water.

Various American communities are also venturing into trying this "new" source of water. One of them, Santee, California, a town located near San Diego, used it to solve the problem of providing water for four recreational lakes. At first the lakes were limited to boating, but gradually, as it was proved that the water in them is pure, the lakes were stocked with fish, and swimming was permitted.

"The idea of swimming in reclaimed sewage water was pretty repulsive at first," admits a typical Santee resident, "but you soon get over it—you just don't think about it. Certainly you can't *tell* the difference. The water is clear and sparkling."

A government study of the Santee use of water states:

This demonstration that the public will knowingly and intimately associate with water reclaimed from sewage in a carefully planned and maintained facility is considered a major project accomplishment. . . . The importance of the Santee experience is that it was needed, it was successful and it was accomplished with a scientific endeavor that was in tune with the current space age era, where everything seems possible.

By 1975, it is estimated, several hundred communities in the United States, and many hundreds more in other parts of the world, will reuse sewage effluent in one way or another. Perhaps much of the use will be for industry, irrigation and recreational lakes, but any use at all of water now wasted will be a gain—not only in adding to our water supplies but in fighting pollution as well.

The reuse of water by industry presents fewer problems than does recycling domestic sewage, and this is an area where the most spectacular gains in water usage can be made. While U.S. homes will give off 30 billion gallons of sewage a day by 1975, industry will use a staggering 250 billion gallons of water every day! Reuse of half that water is a goal that many engineers think can readily be reached.

Others believe that it is not too much to hope for a 75 per cent reusage. They point to accomplishments such as those at a steel plant where the requirements for making a ton of steel were cut from the national average of 65,000 gallons to a net loss of 1,400 gallons. Of course, this was water used for cooling, but many types of plants using water in processes that contaminate it have made great strides toward cleaning it up and reusing it. One typical chemical plant that had been using 100,000 gallons a day cut this to 10,000.

Tapping Underground Water

One day in 1969 geologists exploring for oil in the Libyan desert made a remarkable discovery. All around them lay arid wasteland, mile upon mile of sand dotted by only an occasional oasis. Yet when the drills went down they struck not oil but water. Just 25 to 75 feet under the sun-seared surface of the desert, wherever the geologists drilled, they hit water.

Later they concluded that they had tapped into a vast underground lake—one that covered an area of 1,000 square miles. They estimated that this concealed, untapped reservoir out there in the desert contains an amount of water equal to the flow of the Nile for 1,000 years!

Geologists exploring desert regions of Africa have discovered huge underground rivers beneath the sands of barren lands.

Actually, the discovery was not as surprising to the geologists as it seems to the layman, for hydrologists know that much of the world's supply of fresh water is underground. The surface water that provides us with most of our supply of water today is only ⅓ of 1 per cent of the fresh water on earth. Ground water, on the other hand, makes up 25 per cent of the total—more than 75 times as much.

In the form of underground natural reservoirs, called aquifers, this groundwater exists under many parts of the world. Beneath New Jersey, for instance, there is a vast supply of 20 trillion gallons. The gigantic Snake River Plains Aquifer in Idaho covers an area of 12,000 square miles and contains over 300 cubic miles of water. This is more than the total rainfall of the western plains of the United States in a century. An even bigger aquifer than the one beneath the Libyan desert runs under the Sahara. It covers an area of more than 116,000 square miles. The largest in the United States is the Atlantic and Gulf Coastal Plain Aquifer, extending from Massachusetts to the Mexican border. In places it is 500 miles wide.

There are even great aquifers under the oceans, as oceanographers recently discovered when they were drilling off the East coast of Florida. From an underground pool they tapped, fresh water shot up, through a pipe, 30 feet into the air above the sea's surface.

Where does all this water come from?

One of the sources is surface water. Rainfall and seepage from rivers and lakes percolates downward until it meets what is called the water table, the top of the underground water. It is estimated that a billion gallons of water a day from this source pour into the underground water resources of Long Island, New York.

A second source is "juvenile water," created by the immense pressures and heat deep underground. These set up chemical processes which change hydrogen and oxygen in the rocks into water. Hydrologists can only guess at how much of this new water there might be, but they theorize that the amount of such water being constantly added to world resources is very great.

A third source is "connate water," water which geologists believe was trapped millions of years ago in folds of rocks as the earth was convulsed by geological upheavals.

These underground resources are certain to become more important in providing water for tomorrow's world. In the United States, we already extract one-fourth of all the water we use from the ground, and experts estimate that as we gain knowledge of ground water and improve techniques for extracting it, this percentage can be greatly increased.

"You can't use it if you can't find it," is a remark commonly made by geologists. Finding underground water is a task which hundreds of scientists all over the world are tackling. They have many new tools for scientific water witching that enable them to "see" into the ground. One of them, seismic sounding, uses man-made earthquakes. Explosive charges near the surface are set off and the vibrations picked up by seismographic instruments at various distances from the explosion point. The speed and nature of the vibrations indicates the composition of the rocks through which they pass. By interpreting the seismographic readings, scientists can determine the presence of water.

Using another technique, hydrologists send electrical impulses through the ground from one instrument to another set up some distance away. Measurement of the resistance of the earth through which the current passes can show the presence of water. Water-bearing rocks present less resistance than dry ones. By plotting the path of the currents, an underground water deposit or aquifer can be outlined.

Still another way of finding water is to use radioactive tracers. By injecting harmless isotopes into the ground at given points, and then sampling the earth at distant points where their presence will be revealed, the direction and rate of flow of an aquifer can be determined. The water in some aquifers has thus been revealed to move at only a few inches a day. Others may move at several hundred yards a day. In no aquifer does water move at anything like the speed it does in above-the-ground rivers.

Valuable as these and a number of other techniques may be, the water seekers still depend on drills as basic tools. One of these is a device known as the "continuous flight auger," a simple kind of drill that can be mounted on a light truck or jeep and operated by one man. It drills easily to depths of 300 feet at a cost of less than 50¢ a foot. It has been used to plot many aquifers close to the surface.

In many parts of the world, ancient wells which yielded a limited amount of water are replaced by new wells that tap abundant underground sources.

Drilling for deeper aquifers requires drills of the type used in the oil industry. These powerful drills can penetrate 10,000 feet or more, but are not generally economical for water drilling. However, hydrologists often get a bonus from the drilling activities of oil prospectors, who turn over core samples and instrument readings to the water scientists, as they did in the case of the huge aquifer discovered in the Libyan desert.

It may take some time before we have a complete map of the world's underground water resources, but enough of them have been mapped to encourage the scientific opinion that, even if all other sources of water should fail, we could turn to these hidden rivers under the earth. In fact, one estimate puts these resources at 8,000 times the present annual usage of water.

Scientists are hopeful that we'll find other ways to use underground water than by simply drilling wells down to it. They believe we may make wide use of a technique developed by pioneering Israeli engineers, who have employed aquifers to move water from one place to another. In the 1950s, hydrologists observed an alarming drop in the flow of springs and wells in much of Israel. They knew what that meant; the water table was dropping because of the rising demand for water in that growing country. There was plenty of water in the northern part of the country, in Lake Tiberius (called the Sea of Galilee in Biblical times). How could they deliver some of it to the places where it was needed? They calculated that a surface canal would lose too much water by evaporation and that it would have to be concrete-lined to prevent absorption by the thirsty sands through which it would pass. The cost of delivering the water would be so high that it could not be used for agricultural purposes.

The solution? Why not use an aquifer? Geologists knew that water-bearing rocks ran without a break from north to south in their country. Engineers simply pumped water out of Lake Tiberius, conveying it to nearby wells. Sure enough, in a few months, the level of wells in the south began to rise. The aquifer served as a vast underground pipe that cost nothing to build and lost no water through evaporation.

One of the greatest obstacles to using underground water is the fact that much of it is brackish—that is, it contains quantities of minerals and salts. Hydrologists estimate that two-thirds of the water underlying the

United States is somewhat brackish, having from 1,000 to 3,000 parts per million of salts. However, they are not dismayed by the condition of this water. They have plenty of evidence that it can be desalted by some of the same methods that promise to unlock the greatest water treasure trove of all—the salty oceans of the world.

Turning Salt Water into Fresh

Remember those staggering figures about the contents of the world's oceans: *3,700,000 cubic miles, containing 97.2 per cent of all the water on our planet!* Unfortunately, for a thirsty world in desperate need of water, it also contains all that salt—so much that, if it were extracted and spread evenly, it would cover the entire land surface of the earth to a depth of 40 feet! No matter how successful we may be in finding other sources of water, it seems certain that, to get enough, we will have to find large-scale ways to tap this immense resource.

Engineers have developed many promising approaches to this greatest of all water challenges. A basic one is a modern form of an old method—distillation. Aristotle developed a system of distilling sea water for shipboard use, and it is probable that the system was used long before the Greek philosopher worked out his scheme.

Distillation is a matter of applying heat to water so that vapor rises from it. Let this vapor condense on a cold surface, and you have pure distilled water, freed of salts and minerals. It works out very simply on a small scale; the problem is to make it work in big installations. Engineers have been trying to devise practical distillation

Most of the world's water is in the oceans. We must tap them to meet the water needs of tomorrow.

systems for a long time. In fact, back in 1883, Charles Wilson, a mining engineer, found himself faced with a baffling water problem. Assigned to develop a mine high in the Andes of Chile, he discovered that the wells produced only brackish water, undrinkable by the miners and the mules that hauled the ore. It seemed that the large quantities of water needed would have to be hauled up steep mountain grades at great expense.

The ingenious engineer decided to put the bright mountain sunlight to work. He ordered the building of a huge wooden framework, covering 50,000 square feet. On this framework he set sheets of window glass, making what looked like an immense greenhouse. Into the space under the glass he pumped the brackish water from the wells. The heat of the sun caused some of this water to evaporate. When it did, the vapor condensed on the underside of the glass. From there it ran down and dripped into troughs which carried it to a tank. The miners had plenty of fresh, drinkable water.

This scheme works out very well on small installations, and is used today in many parts of the world. The difficulty in using the heat of the sun is that huge surfaces have to be employed to gather enough heat. This calls for so many materials and so much land space that the effect of getting "free" heat from the sun is cancelled out. If other kinds of fuel are used installations can be smaller, but the cost of fuel—coal, oil or gas—may be prohibitive.

Engineers are working on more efficient ways to use the distillation principle. In one of them, called multiflash distillation, the salt water is subjected to a series of quick heat and pressure changes which cause it to flash into steam very fast, speeding up the whole process.

Other systems that hold great promise are being tried in many parts of the world. In one of them, oddly enough, cold instead of heat is used. The idea behind this is that it takes less energy to freeze sea water than it does to boil it. In experimental systems, sea water enters at 60-75° F. and passes through a device that removes air, through heat exchangers, where it is cooled further, and then into a freezing chamber, where it is converted into a slurry. (Sea water freezes at 27° F.) The slurry is pumped from the freezer to a washer, where the brine is separated and ice crystals washed free of salt. Then the ice is scraped into a melter.

Another system, called electrodialysis, takes the salt out of the water, rather than the water out of the salt,

One approach to desalting water. This small-scale plant, which takes the salt out of 10,000 gallons of water a day, heralds bigger plants to come.

At the start of the 1970s, this was the world's largest water desalination plant. It processes 7,500,000 gallons a day for Tijuana, Mexico.

as in the distillation processes. Salts, when dissolved, take the form of positively or negatively charged ions. Sodium, for instance, becomes a positively charged ion, chloride a negatively charged one. Electrodialysis uses "sandwiches" of membranes—ones permeable by positively charged ions are alternated with ones permeable by negatively charged ions. When an electric current is applied, the salts pass through the membranes, leaving salt-depleted water in the middle.

Still another system, reverse osmosis, holds much promise. If you have a weak solution separated from a stronger solution by a permeable membrane, fluid will move into the stronger solution and build up pressure there. This is osmosis, the same process that is at work in the cells of animals and plants. The pressure that is induced in a particular solution is known as its osmotic pressure. Research is being directed to reversing the process, forcing pure water out of solution by confining it within a semipermeable membrane and applying a pressure greater than its natural osmotic pressure.

The problem with all these systems is their high cost, arising both from the basic plant and the large amount of energy required. In the California town of Coalinga, where drinking water was once hauled in at a cost of $7.50 a thousand gallons, water at 80¢ a thousand gallons from a desalting plant seemed cheap. However, to an industry using vast quantities of water, 15¢ a thousand gallons would seem expensive.

By building pilot plants of different sizes, many research organizations are testing out the various systems, hoping to find a way to turn the salt water of the sea

Artist's visualization of a huge nuclear desalting plant of the future. It could provide all the water and all the power required by a city of 5,000,000.

and brackish inland waters into fresh water at costs that compare favorably with that of water from other sources. Some say that 10¢ a thousand gallons is not an impossible dream.

The researchers know for sure that, whatever the system used, desalination plants of the future will have to be big. The largest plant in the world in 1970 is an experimental one in Tijuana, Mexico, producing 7½ million gallons a day. Five times larger than any such plant ever built, it will be dwarfed by a giant new plant being constructed on the Gulf of California in a joint venture of the U.S. Government, the Mexican Government and the International Atomic Energy Commission. When it is completed, sometime in the 1970s, it will have a capacity of *one billion gallons* a day!

7

TRANSPORTING WATER by LAND, AIR and SEA

"The greatest engineering project ever conceived."

That is the description that may well be applied to a bold plan to remodel the rivers of North America. To carry it out, engineers propose to take the waters of the mighty Yukon and other northern rivers and send them down a system of rivers and canals clear to Mexico.

A wild dream? Not at all, say the planners of NAWAPA (The North American Water and Power Alliance), a scheme for solving the fresh-water problems of our continent in the world of tomorrow. They are sure that the project is not only practical but a necessity if we are to get the water we will need for home use, industry and agriculture.

The Map Changers

Before examining future possibilities let's look at some of the map-changing projects already under way in the early '70s. There are many of them, in different parts of the world, all having the same objective—to get water from places where it isn't needed to places where it is.

The idea of bringing water from a distance is certainly not new. In ancient Egypt, around 2500 B.C., a freshwater canal was built from Cairo to Suez. In 691 B.C., the ruler of Nineveh built an aqueduct from a dam on the River Zab, 50 miles away, to provide water for the flourishing city. About the same time, the Greeks were building aqueducts, including one that called for constructing a tunnel 3,000 feet long.

The Romans were the supreme builders of aqueducts in the ancient world. Starting with the first Aqua Appia in 312 B.C., they built up a network of aqueducts with a total mileage of 381 miles, capable of supplying the city of Rome with 130,000,000 gallons of water a day.

There was a long break in the building of such water systems in the Middle Ages until, in 1613, the English constructed what might be called the first aqueduct of the modern era. It carried water to London from springs in Hertfordshire, 38 miles away. Before that, late in the 1500s, Sir Francis Drake, of Plymouth, built a 24-mile-long canal to carry water to the city of which he was then mayor.

In the United States the first large long-distance water-conveying system was the Croton Aqueduct, started in

1842. Like the New River Aqueduct serving London, it was 38 miles long. In 1913, the Catskill Aqueduct, also serving New York City, was completed. It ran for 120 miles, delivering half a billion gallons of water a day from the mountains after which it is named. In that same year, California topped that distance with its Owens River Aqueduct, carrying water to Los Angeles from the east slope of the Sierra Nevada, 233 miles away. Another California engineering feat was accomplished in 1939 when the immense Colorado Aqueduct, a giant pipe that ran over 250 miles from the Colorado River, started delivering a billion gallons of water a day to southern California.

All these projects of the past are dwarfed by the map-changing ventures of today, and the even mightier ones planned for tomorrow. The biggest one actually under way in 1970 is the California State Water Plan. This $13 billion project calls for a system of canals, tunnels and pipes that will convey the waters of rivers in the copiously watered northern part of the state to the dry southern part. The Feather River Aqueduct, the first to be completed, will be 735 miles long, easily the longest in the world. Among the engineering feats required to complete it is the pumping of the water from sea level to an altitude of 3,000 feet to get over Tehachapi Pass, which divides northern from southern California.

On other continents, great water diversion projects are also under way. One of them, to be completed by 1975, is the Snowy Mountains Scheme in Australia. To carry it out, engineers are building a system of dams that will

The Snowy River Scheme is an immense water diversion project in Australia. It involved building 80 miles of tunnels and 200 miles of aqueducts to bring water to arid regions.

turn around two rivers, the Snowy and the Murrumbidgee, to make them flow through dry country instead of across the regions of plentiful rainfall which they now traverse.

On another continent is the vast Indus River Project, a joint undertaking of India and West Pakistan. It affects six major rivers, which will be made to flow through more than 400 miles of canals into a system of reservoirs.

Rivaling NAWAPA in scope is the Soviet's Ob-Yenisei project. This calls for reversing the flow of two mighty rivers, the Ob and the Yenisei, which now run north, carrying vast quantities of water the wrong way. Wrong, that is, from the standpoint of agriculturalists, who would like to find a way to water the arid central steppes to the south.

The planners have figured out that, by putting a dam across the Ob at a certain point, they could create a huge inland sea, as large as the entire country of Italy. A similar dam across the Yenisei would create another, although smaller, man-made lake. The two lakes could then be linked by canal. The water in this system would flow westward and southward, clear to the Aral and Caspian Seas, through a canal which would, in effect, become a giant new river.

NAWAPA—Water from the Far North

NAWAPA is breathtaking in its scope. It would affect the water supplies of Los Angeles, Chicago, New York, Toronto—almost every large U.S. and Canadian city. It would turn 40,000,000 dry acres in the United States into fertile food-raising land, and do the same for 10,000,000 acres in Canada. It would provide water for arid Mexico, permitting the irrigation of eight times as much land as that watered by the mighty Aswan Dam project in Egypt. It would solve a vast number of water problems, raise the level of the Great Lakes, increase the flow of sluggish rivers and provide huge amounts of power.

The dream of remaking the water system of an entire continent first took shape in the mind of Donald McCord Baker, a planning engineer for the city of Los Angeles. At the time, in the early '50s, Baker had been working on plans to bring water from northern California to the dry southern part of the state. If the principle of diverting a river to supply another part of a state was workable, why couldn't the same idea be applied on a larger scale? Like bringing water from rivers in Canada and Alaska south to the continental United States, even to Mexico?

When Baker studied the map, his dream soared. What caught his attention was the Rocky Mountain Trench, a tremendous gorge that runs through the Canadian Rockies and extends into Montana. He suddenly saw this 500-mile-long trough as a storage reservoir. At its altitude of 3,000 feet, water could come tumbling out of the giant reservoir to drain southward.

Where would water to fill the gorge come from? There are many rivers in British Columbia—the Peace, the Kootenay and, of course, the Columbia—all flowing to the Pacific. And to the north, in Alaska, there are three great rivers—the Yukon, the Tanana and the Susitna, all draining into the Pacific, where their water is lost for man's use. What if these rivers were turned around and made to flow into the Trench?

The idea was awesome, certainly too big for one man. Its development would require the work of many engineers. Baker turned to the Ralph M. Parsons Company, an engineering firm which had worked on a variety of major projects in many parts of the world. The company engineers admitted that they were staggered by the scope of the project, but, as they explored it further, they concluded that it was a sound, practical possibility and proceeded to draw up some detailed plans for what they decided to call The North American Water and Power Alliance.

As the scheme developed over the years, the NAWAPA

proposal lost none of its grandeur. As currently outlined it calls for building a series of dams near the headwaters of the three Alaska rivers and the Peace River in Canada. From a system of reservoirs back of these dams water would flow into the giant artificial lake in the Rocky Mountain Trench. Some of this water would be channeled by canal through the western United States, following the mountain contours clear to Mexico, to flow into the Rio Grande and the Yaqui River. Aqueducts would branch off this main canal to serve California, Colorado, Arizona and New Mexico. An eastern branch, the Canadian–Great Lakes Seaway Canal, would flow toward the Great Lakes, reaching Lake Superior through a linking of natural lakes by canals.

The engineering problems are enormous. For instance, one of the dams will have to be 1,700 feet high. A single 80-foot-in-diameter tunnel would be 50 miles long. Building the canals calls for moving 45 billion cubic yards of earth. Structures in the project would require 70 million tons of steel. A work force of several thousand men would have to toil for 10 to 20 years, and the total cost might run as high as $100,000,000.

However, much of the cost of both construction and operation would be paid for by the enormous amounts of power produced by hydroelectric plants in the various dams. As the waters descend to sea level, they would be capable of producing enough energy to provide 30,000,000 kilowatts for Canadian use, 38,000,000 kilowatts for the United States.

One of the most remarkable benefits of NAWAPA

would be the new navigational route opened up. The project would actually make it possible for ships to cross North America from the Atlantic to the Pacific!

Will this colossus of engineering projects ever be built? Various governmental agencies in the United States and Canada have investigated it and opinion is divided. One objection is that it is too expensive. Another one, raised by many Canadians, is the utilization of what is essentially an invaluable Canadian resource for largely United States use. Others question the desirability of flooding the immense Rocky Mountain Trench.

However, many think these objections are not serious ones in view of the desperate need for more water that will confront us in tomorrow's world. They point out that the $100,000,000 is only 25 per cent more than the United States spent in a single year on its military budget during the Vietnam war. The flooding of a large area in Canada would, these supporters maintain, be offset by the recreational possibilities of such a huge body of water.

NAWAPA certainly deserves the serious study it is receiving in the three countries that would be affected by this greatest of engineering projects.

The GRAND Plan to Meet Water Shortages

Not so grand as the NAWAPA project is one which bears the name GRAND, for Great Replenishment and Northern Development—a scheme which would provide huge new water supplies for a large section of eastern Canada and the eastern and midwestern United States.

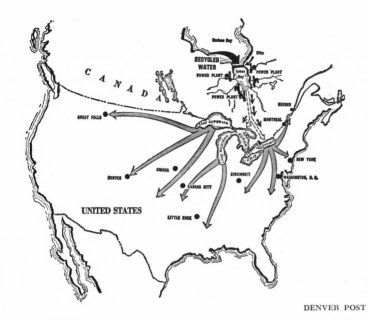

The **GRAND** Plan for water diversion would replenish the Great Lakes and provide new water supplies for much of the central and eastern United States.

Developed by a Canadian engineer, Thomas W. Kierans, GRAND calls for building a dam across James Bay, which extends south from Hudson Bay. While at present this is an arm of the sea, containing salty water, it is fed by a number of rivers. When dammed, sea water would be shut out and the flow of the rivers into James Bay would gradually turn it into a freshwater lake.

The engineers would encounter a slight obstacle that would have to be overcome before this water could be made to flow south. There is a divide in the land, south of the bay, which rises 1,000 feet. Immense pumps would be needed to carry the water over this hump to another reservoir. From there it would flow downhill to the Great Lakes, the surfaces of which are some 300 feet lower. Power to lift the water over the rise would be provided by hydroelectric plants on the rivers feeding into James Bay. They would also provide a surplus of energy which could be used for industrial development of this far northern region, which is so rich in natural resources.

The effect of the new system would be to supply an abundance of water that could replenish any taken from the Great Lakes, which would serve as immense reservoirs. Many of Canada's people live along the Great Lakes and the St. Lawrence Seaway, and in the United States, 35 per cent of the population live in the eight states bordering the Great Lakes. By the year 2000, one water study indicates, the states around lakes Superior, Michigan and Huron alone will need 23.4 billion gallons of water a day more than the rivers and the Great Lakes can provide. The GRAND plan could supply all necessary water, since the amount sent into the system from James Bay could be regulated according to needs. In dry years, when the level of the Great Lakes would fall and the rivers run low, more water would be admitted. In wet years it would be reduced.

The engineer who conceived the GRAND idea sees it as a powerful weapon against pollution. The new water could be used all along the Great Lakes system to "flush out" pockets of pollution by the use of rivers and canals. While a canal filled with polluted water could be a problem in itself, "moving water," says Kierans, "is easier to deal with than stagnant water."

The Long Island Sound Project

Water engineers looking around New York City for new sources of supply to meet the growing needs of this megalopolis, and prevent for all time a water famine recurrence like that of the '60s, studied Long Island Sound, the arm of the sea that lies north of Long Island between the Connecticut and New York shores. Too bad that nature hadn't seen fit to make this body of water into a freshwater lake. What a splendid source of water it would be!

As he indulged in this bit of very wishful thinking, Dr. Robert D. Gerard, of Columbia University's Lamont Geological Observatory, was struck by a bold thought. Maybe nature hadn't done it—but perhaps man could. Of course, the water in the Sound was salty, but couldn't that be changed?

The key to the scheme that took shape on the drawing boards of engineers and hydrologists requires the building of just two dams. One would be at the western end, at the East River. Another dam, at the eastern end, would run from the northeastern tip of Long Island to the Connecticut shore, east of the mouth of the Connecticut River. Building these dams would impound nearly 42,000,000 acre-feet of water. At first, the water would be salty, but gradually, as water from the Connecticut, the Housatonic and many other rivers flowed into it, the water would become fresh, making the "lake" an immense reservoir which could supply all the needs of the New York area—which will be three times greater by the year 2000 than they are today.

The plan seems to be completely practical and relatively cheap. Estimates of cost run from $2 billion to $3 billion. Proceeds from the sale of water, even at very low costs, and tolls, which would be collected from traffic over the highways that would be built atop the dams, would enable the project literally to pay for itself. It presents no formidable engineering problems. Although the eastern dam would become the longest in the United States, it would still be only half the length of the dam which engineers in the Netherlands built to seal off the Zuider Zee. To permit shipping in the Lake, if that seemed desirable, sea-level locks could readily be built in the dams.

Rivers in the Sky

Many places indicated on today's maps as arid lands may, in the future, be shown as fertile regions. Barren plains may become tilled fields yielding crops to feed an overpopulated, hungry world. Small streams may become rivers. Rivers that now run dry may flow the year round.

These are expectations of scientists who hope to make better use of nature's aerial water transport system. As moisture evaporates from the oceans and other bodies of water, it is constantly on the move, in the form of clouds. The trick is to make them drop more of their water in places where it is needed. In the United States, Canada, Australia and many other countries, scientists have already turned rainmaking into a practical tool for increasing water resources. Once a pseudoscience scoffed at by reputable scientists, rainmaking has been the subject of a quarter of a century of scientific research.

The breakthrough came when a young General Electric scientist, Vincent Schaefer, made a discovery that

ENVIRONMENTAL SCIENCE SERVICES ADMISTRATION

Photographs sent to earth by satellites are used by rainmakers
to learn in advance of favorable cloud conditions.

opened up the possibility of making rain to order. With Dr. Irving Langmuir, Schaefer had been working on problems of airplane icing and had found that when ice crystals are introduced into clouds that are "supercooled" —that is, having temperatures far below freezing—the water droplets in the cloud evaporate and ice crystals grow. Water then condenses on the crystals until they get so heavy that they fall, as rain or snow. Schaefer had the idea that he ought to be able to carry out laboratory experiments in creating ice crystals. He breathed into a deep-freezing unit and produced a "cloud"—just as he had been sure he would. Now to produce some ice crystals. He dropped various substances into the freezer. No crystals.

Perhaps, he reasoned, the unit wasn't cold enough. How could he make it colder than the greatest cold it could produce—a temperature of $-23°$ C.? Dry ice, with its temperature of $-70°$ C., should do the job. It produced the lower temperature, all right, but, to the researcher's astonishment, it did much more. When he dropped the dry ice into the box, a multitude of ice crystals suddenly appeared.

Next, he decided, he would try dropping dry ice from an airplane into actual clouds—an experiment that was carried out on November 13, 1946. Flying in a rented plane that took off from the Schenectady, N.Y., airport, Schaefer released three pounds of dry ice by opening the window and letting the slipstream pull it out. Looking behind the plane, he had the thrill of seeing it glistening with billions of crystals. And below the clouds, snow began to fall. It did not reach the ground, but the jubilant scientist knew that he had proved that clouds could be made to give up their moisture. The dry ice cooled the cloud so that ice crystals formed. At last the old dream of man-created rain was a reality.

Since that historic day many successful experiments in rainmaking have been carried out, and new techniques have been developed, but the principle is that discovered by Langmuir and Schaefer. The major change is the substitution of silver iodide for the dry ice that Schaefer used. Shortly after the first cloud-seeding experiment, an associate of these two rainmaking pioneers, Bernard Vonnegut, discovered that silver iodide had a structure like that of ice crystals. Water droplets would attach themselves to these crystals as readily as they would to those of natural ice.

The silver iodide is distributed in the atmosphere by generators in planes or on the ground. In mountainous areas, generators placed properly in relationship to wind currents can cover a wide area. These generators are simply small furnaces that produce silver iodide smoke.

Another device recently developed is called "Weathercord." It consists of a length of detonating fuse impregnated with a mixture of explosive and silver iodide. When dropped from a plane at altitudes of 17,000 to 22,000 feet, and timed to explode at desired cloud levels, it delivers billions of silver iodide particles right into the heart of a moisture-laden cloud.

This was the method used in a spectacular rainmaking success in Iran. In 1967, a prolonged drought struck the northern part of the country. Reservoirs were drying up and crops dying in parched fields that no longer received the irrigation water they must have to grow in that dry land. The city of Teheran faced a critical water shortage.

In 1968, the rainmakers moved in. Their target was an area of 4,375 square miles, a mountainous region much like many areas in the western part of the United States. They were able to use a new tool for spotting cloud formations suitable for seeding. Orbiting the earth in space, ESSA and Nimbus weather satellites take photographs of the earth. Coded electronically, these photos are sent to receiving stations in many countries. In Iran, the weathermen set up a special station, where they received as many as 16 photographs a day showing movements of clouds over the entire Middle East. By studying these photos, scientists were alerted well in advance that promising clouds were moving their way.

As the planes roared into the favorable formations, rain began to fall on Iran. In a few months, the empty reservoirs in the Elburz Mountains filled up, some of them actually running over. The drought was ended for a country that had literally been drying up. In 1969 and 1970, the performance was repeated, with more than 100 per cent increases above normal rainfall. A country in which 80 per cent of the population is engaged in farming 11 per cent of the land is looking forward to the opening up of new farmlands that can be watered by the abundance of water extracted from the sky.

There have been many triumphs for the rainmakers on a less spectacular scale. The most significant operations have been aimed at increasing the snowpack. For example, during one recent winter, farmers on the western slope of the Colorado Rockies knew early in the season that there was trouble ahead. The snowpack that would feed the streams and fill the reservoirs later in the year was far below normal. Rainmakers set up batteries of silver iodide generators in the mountains that were so short of snow. The clouds, which had been moving past without dropping their moisture, responded. In a single month the snowpack increased 100 per cent. Nearby areas not affected by the generators had snow, too, but only half as much as the seeded area. The drought was averted.

Increasing the snowpack is the object of the largest rainmaking experiment ever launched. Through Project Skywater, scientists of the U.S. Bureau of Reclamation hope to pour billions of gallons of water into the Colorado River. The project, which will end in 1973, requires setting up hundreds of generators, flying thousands of monitoring flights and making detailed hour-by-hour studies of the results. The scientists will be disappointed if, when they add everything up in 1973 or 1974, they cannot report a 20 per cent increase in the snowfall that feeds the Colorado. That would add almost 700 billion gallons of water to the great western river that is a vital source of water for seven states. It would also be a major milestone on the road to tapping "the rivers in the sky."

As a Project Skywater scientist points out, "More water passes over the Colorado River Basin in clouds every *week* than the river produces in runoff in a *year*. If we

A promising cloud before seeding . . . begins to billow and ex-

pand as silver iodide is released in it. A heavy rainfall results.

can tap only a couple of days worth of skywater, we'll be happy."

Water from Icebergs

Icebergs to provide water for coastal regions? It sounds like some fantastic science fiction scheme, but actually it is not a wild idea at all. It may prove to be a way of conveying water long distances. For years scientists have looked longingly at the ice-covered Antarctic. No less than 80 per cent of the world's supply of fresh water is locked in this vast ice cap in the Southern Hemisphere. Each year hundreds of icebergs break off the glaciers that cover the frozen continent and float away. One iceberg as large as the entire state of Rhode Island was once sighted by the Navy. While most do not run that big, there are many that cover hundreds of square miles. Scientists calculate that even an average-sized iceberg would contain over 200 billion gallons of water.

What a rare prize such a monstrous ice cube made of fresh water would be if, instead of simply dissolving in southern seas, it could somehow be brought to one of the water-short regions of the world!

Dr. John Isaacs, of the Scripps Institute of Oceanography, one of the first to seriously propose using icebergs for water supplies, calculates that a "small" iceberg with a volume of one cubic mile would contain 3½ million acre-feet of water. This would be enough to provide for the needs of 3½-million families for a year! At 10¢ per 1,000 gallons, a low price for water, such an iceberg would be worth $100,000,000.

Can icebergs from the Antarctic provide fresh water for distant
coastal cities? Scientists are studying that possibility.

But could an iceberg actually be moved thousands of miles from the Antarctic to regions that need water? Since Dr. Isaacs described the possibility, several years ago, two American scientists have devoted much attention to the practical details. The approach of Dr. William Campbell, a hydrologist with the U.S. Geological Survey, and Dr. Wilford Weeks, a glaciologist of the U.S. Army's Cold Regions Research and Engineering Laboratory, was to divide the problem into three parts. Where could a suitable supply of icebergs be found? How much power would be required to transport them? How much ice would melt on the long voyages?

For a source, they settled on the Ross, Amery and Filchner ice shelves of Antarctica. Here they found that, of the icebergs breaking off from the immense glaciers, many were of the best shape for towing—long and flat so they would not roll or capsize. Such an iceberg would have about 83 per cent of its bulk beneath the surface. There would be no trouble finding plenty that met the specifications. Observational satellites could readily spot the most likely prospects at any given time.

When the scientists calculated the amount of energy needed to move an iceberg containing some 207 billion gallons of water, they first checked out the possibility of using a large number of tugs. Eventually, they decided that one 8,000-horsepower tug, traveling at one knot an hour, could do the job. More tugs could move faster, but would be less economical. Dr. Isaacs has advanced the idea that ocean currents and winds might take over most of the job. He proposes that icebergs be towed into ocean

currents moving in the right direction and that economical sail-driven tugs, taking advantage of favorable winds, could make possible speeds of two or three knots.

How much water would the icebergs lose? A lot, of course. Campbell and Weeks figure that by the time one had been delivered to the coast of northwest Australia, a distance of some 3,200 miles, it would have lost 86 per cent of its starting bulk. It would cost about $1,000,000 to tow a small iceberg, one 250 yards thick and 2,700 yards across, that distance, but on arrival it would still contain $5,500,000 worth of water at a low 10¢ per 1,000 gallons.

There would be no problem of getting the water ashore once the iceberg reached its destination. The water from the melting ice would float on top of the

Navy craft experiment with pushing a vast chunk of ice. Movement of such an iceberg over long distances would be helped by favorable ocean currents.

heavier sea water and pipes run out from land could pump it into reservoirs, water systems and irrigation canals.

Icebergs could be a practical way to alleviate the water shortage in many parts of the world, and could have an important effect on the food supply of developing nations. As Dr. Isaacs points out, "In the Southern Hemisphere, at least, the great Antarctic bergs are pointed at the entries to natural highways (ocean currents) that lead to the deserts of Africa, Australia and South America."

Probably these will be the places where iceberg water will first be delivered. However, hydrologists don't rule out the possibility that ice from the Antarctic could be used to supply fresh water to Los Angeles and other cities on the west coast of the United States. You may some day be drinking the water of an iceberg from the far-off Antarctic!

THE OUTLOOK for CLEAN AIR and CLEAN WATER

There are many ways to fight pollution and to tap new water resources. As we have seen, science has developed an arsenal of weapons that hold promise of future success in cleaning up our environment. Whether we will actually achieve this goal is a question that science and engineering alone cannot answer. To be sure, finding the tools to fight pollution is the task of science. But it is the responsibility of society—of all citizens—to put the tools to work.

A start has been made, in the form of laws that crack down on polluters. National clean air and clean water acts, as well as many state laws, are on the books—and they are working. It was under such a law that the oil company responsible for the 1970 oil spill off Louisiana was fined one million dollars.

In many states, citizens have the right to bring suit against industries that permit pollutants to pour from their smokestacks or poison the waters near their plants. Even governmental agencies are not free from responsibility. The U.S. Navy has been sued by the State of California for dumping refuse from ships into San Diego harbor, thus violating the Federal Water Pollution Control Act.

To make attacks on pollution more effective, a new Federal agency was set up in 1970. The Environmental Protection Agency, with broad powers and ample funds, is charged with coordinating previously scattered efforts.

However, important though they are, national agencies are not enough. In the United Nations and among scientific organizations there are serious discussions about the need for international laws to cope with the problems of ocean pollution and fouled air that moves from one country to another.

"There is no escape from the responsibility of planetary management," says U Thant, United Nations Secretary General. We must, he asserts, create an international environmental authority if we have any hopes of avoiding the disaster of "a civilization which has run out of air, water, resources, and food."

Laws, and organizations to enforce them, are important, but the greatest need is money—huge amounts of it. Studies show that the United States alone will have to spend as much as a *trillion dollars* in the next decade if we hope to really control air and water pollution and provide the abundance of water we will need. The vast research programs, the maintenance of law enforcement agencies, the monitoring systems, the new sewage and water treatment plants, the changes in automobiles, represent a total cost far beyond anything we have ever spent on peacetime projects.

Where will all this money come from? Obviously, from the people. Everyone is going to have to help pay for clean air and clean water in the form of higher taxes and higher prices on nearly all the goods that we buy.

"There is no way to avoid the costs of pollution. Either we put up with the more and more costly consequences, or we accept the costs of pollution prevention and control. This is the stark either-or of the situation. There is no other choice."

So reads a report of the Federal Water Quality Administration. Offhand, few would quarrel with the need to spend the money that it takes to fight pollution. However, there is still general public unwillingness to face up to just how high that cost can be.

In a survey conducted by the Gallup Organization for the National Wildlife Federation, some remarkable attitudes were discovered. Asked if they would be willing to pay $2 a month extra on their electricity bills to stop air and water pollution by power plants, a resounding 77 per cent of the people in the sampling replied that they would *not* pay this amount. How about $1 a month? A few more thought they would go along with that, but 62 per cent still said they would not. So how about a much smaller sum—just $3 a year, a mere 25¢ a month? A substantial number—30 per cent—replied that they would not be happy about paying even that much!

Questions asked about amounts that people would be

willing to pay for a *total* attack on *all* forms of pollution were even more revealing. The questions started with $200 a year, a figure many environmentalists consider realistic. How many would be willing to pay out $200 in added taxes and extra costs of food, automobiles, and other manufactured goods, to fight pollution? Only 22 per cent said that they would cheerfully pay out this amount; 32 per cent would accept $100; 42 per cent would pay $50. Only 55 per cent would be willing to pay even $20. Over a third of all people queried indicated that they were opposed to paying anything at all.

Though many ecologists fear that we have started our fight on pollution too late, others are hopeful that if we take action *now* we can overcome the conditions created by our hesitant beginning.

Dr. Barry Commoner, Director of the Center for the Biology of Natural Systems at Washington University, is a noted environmentalist who has sometimes been called a prophet of doom. His many warnings of the dangers confronting us have often sounded pessimistic. Yet Dr. Commoner is hopeful that there is yet time.

"I believe," he said, in 1970,

that we have, as of now, a single decade in which to design the fundamental changes in technology that we must put into effect in the 1980s—if we are to survive. We will need to seize on the decade of the 70s as a period of grace—a decade which must be used for a vast pilot program to guide the coming reconstruction of the nation's system of productivity. This is the urgency of the environmental crisis—we

Clean air and clean water for tomorrow's urbanized world—this is a goal that can be achieved only if science, industry, government and all citizens work together.

must determine now to develop, in the next decade, the new means of our salvation.

How can we possibly accomplish this enormous task? None of us is wise enough to offer a blueprint. Nevertheless, the roles and responsibilities of the various segments of our society can, in a general way, be delineated.

Clearly, an initial responsibility must be undertaken by the community of scientists, engineers, and technologists. New priorities need to be set for basic research and technological development; new types of skills will need to be taught and learned. These needs have already been sensed by our students and by many of their teachers. There has been a sharp awakening in many university classrooms and laboratories to the urgency of the environmental crisis.

We are enormously fortunate that our young people have become particularly sensitive to the threat of environmental catastrophe. Nor is this surprising, for *they* are the first generation in human history to carry strontium-90 in their bones and DDT in their fat; their bodies will record, in time, the effects of the new environmental insults on human health. It is they who face the frightful task of seeking humane knowledge in a world which has, with cunning perversity, transformed the power that knowledge generates into an instrument of catastrophe.

I think that our young people will demonstrate that they are, in fact, equal to this task—as their ecological teach-ins and actions begin to mobilize the knowledge of our schools and universities and the civic zeal of our communities for a real attack on the environmental crisis.

U.S. Government Agencies Concerned with Air Pollution, Water Pollution and Water Resources

Atomic Energy Commission
  Washington, D.C. 20545
Bureau of Reclamation
  Department of the Interior
  Washington, D.C. 20240
Department of Agriculture
  Washington, D.C. 20250
Department of Transportation
  Washington, D.C. 20590
Environmental Protection Agency
  Washington, D.C. 20460
Environmental Science Services Administration
  Rockville, Md. 20852
Federal Water Quality Administration
  Washington, D.C. 20460
Fish and Wildlife Service
  Department of the Interior
  Washington, D.C. 20240
Forest Service
  Department of Agriculture
  Washington, D.C. 20250
Geological Survey
  Department of the Interior
  Washington, D.C. 20242
National Air Pollution Control Administration
  801 N. Randolph St.
  Arlington, Va. 22203
Office of Saline Water
  Department of the Interior
  Washington, D.C. 20240

Public Health Service
  Department of Health, Education and Welfare
  330 Independence Ave. S.W.
  Washington, D.C. 20201
Soil Conservation Service
  Department of Agriculture
  Washington, D.C. 20250

Some Organizations Concerned With Environmental Problems

American Forestry Association
    919 17th St. N.W.
    Washington, D.C. 20006
American Water Works Association
    2 Park Ave.
    New York, N.Y. 10016
The Conservation Foundation
    1250 Connecticut Ave. N.W.
    Washington, D.C. 20036
International Union for Conservation of Nature and
        Natural Resources
    2000 P St. N.W.
    Washington, D.C. 20006
The Izaak Walton League of America
    1326 Waukegan Road
    Glenview, Ill. 60025
John Muir Institute for Environmental Studies
    451 Pacific Ave.
    San Francisco, Calif. 94133
        or
    P.O. Box 11
    Cedar Crest, N.Mex. 87008
National Air Conservation Commission
        of the National Tuberculosis and Respiratory
        Disease Association
    1790 Broadway
    New York, N.Y. 10019
National Audubon Society
    1130 Fifth Ave.
    New York, N.Y. 10028

The Nature Conservancy
  1522 K St. N.W.
  Washington, D.C. 20005
National Parks Association
  1701 18th St. N.W.
  Washington, D.C. 20009
The National Wildlife Federation
  1412 16th St. N.W.
  Washington, D.C. 20036
Scientists Institute for Public Information
  30 E. 68th St.
  New York, N.Y. 10021
The Sierra Club
  1050 Mills Tower
  San Francisco, Calif. 94104
The Wilderness Society
  729 15th St. N.W.
  Washington, D.C. 20005

SUGGESTED FURTHER READINGS

Books About Air Pollution

American Public Health Association. *Guide to the Appraisal and Control of Air Pollution.* American Public Health Association, 1969.

Battan, Louis J. *The Unclean Sky.* Doubleday, 1968.

Carr, Donald E. *Breath of Life.* Norton, 1965.

De Bell, Garrett, ed. *The Environmental Handbook.* Ballantine, 1970.

Edelson, Edward. *The Battle for Clean Air;* Public Affairs Pamphlet No. 403. Public Affairs Committee, 1967.

Lawrence, R. D. *Poison Makers.* Nelson, 1969.

Lewis, Alfred. *Clean the Air!* McGraw-Hill, 1965.

Lewis, Howard R. *With Every Breath You Take.* Crown, 1965.

Linton, Ron M. *Terracide.* Little, Brown, 1970.

National Tuberculosis and Respiratory Disease Association. *Air Pollution Primer.* National Tuberculosis and Respiratory Disease Association, 1969.

Stewart, George R. *Not so Rich as You Think.* Houghton Mifflin, 1968.

Books About Water Pollution

Carr, Donald E. *Death of the Sweet Waters.* Norton, 1966.

De Bell, Garrett, ed. *The Environmental Handbook.* Ballantine, 1970.

Graham, Frank, Jr. *Disaster by Default.* (Evans) Lippincott, 1966.

Herber, Lewis. *Crisis in Our Cities.* Prentice-Hall, 1965.

Lawrence, R. D. *Poison Makers.* Nelson, 1969.

Linton, Ron M. *Terracide.* Little, Brown, 1970.

Stewart, George R. *Not so Rich as You Think.* Houghton Mifflin, 1968.

Books About Water Resources

Battan, Louis. *Harvesting the Clouds*. Doubleday, 1969.
Briggs, Walter P. *The Vital Essence*. Harper & Row, 1967.
Carlisle, Norman. *Riches of the Sea*. Sterling, 1967.
Cunningham, Floyd. *1001 Questions Answered About Water Resources*. Dodd Mead, 1967.
Moss, Frank E. *Water Crisis*, Praeger, 1967.
Overman, Michael. *Water*. Doubleday, 1969.
Popkin, Roy. *Desalination*. Praeger, 1968.

INDEX

ABOUT THE AUTHOR

REED MILLARD is an expert in the field of inventions, whose writing ranges from technical reports to popular magazine articles. His deepest interest is environmental science. He believes, as he has indicated in this book, that science, backed by broad social effort, can provide solutions to the vast problems of pollution that confront us today.

SCIENCE BOOK ASSOCIATES is an organization of writers and technical people active in many areas of science and technology. Their work in the preparation of audio-visual materials and training manuals to be used in science-oriented industry gives the editors an inside look at the developments that will affect tomorrow's world.